The Good Decision Diary

'Anna guides us safely and expertly through our inner dialogue and our outer worlds' Julia Bradbury

'Anna's diary made me feel supported and seen, but crucially, also, gently challenged. Her honest encouraging words prompt a realistic personal accountability with grace and understanding at the core. As always with Anna's writing, it left me feeling uplifted and understood' Ellie Taylor

'Anna provides a transformative approach to personal growth. This book is an essential companion for anyone looking to make meaningful changes with kindness and self-awareness' Zoe Blaskey, founder of Motherkind

'Anna Mathur asks just the right questions to stop us sleepwalking through life, getting what matters most to us front and centre, without the usual self-flagellation. Her prompts and approach help us become our own accountability partner, brainstorming new ways of responding to life and self' Suzy Reading

'A reassuring and comforting read, offering immediately actionable insights. It stands as a guiding star in a world filled with infinite choices and indecision' Emma Reed Turrell

'*The Good Decision Diary* offers a reflective, low-pressure approach to personal growth. It's designed as a daily guide for those looking to untangle habits and better understand their inner voice, with more gentleness than the typical fix-yourself-fast approach' Anne-Laure Le Cunff, neuroscientist and author of *Tiny Experiments*

'Compassionate, real and quietly powerful. Anna gives you permission to stop chasing perfection and instead start making progress that actually sticks' Simon Gilham, author of *Stop Lying to Yourself*

'This book is like a dear, wise friend who knows you, gets you, believes in you and is wholeheartedly committed to helping you grow. Like any dear friend, keep it close' Fiona Buckland

ABOUT THE AUTHOR

Anna Mathur is a psychotherapist and bestselling author. She's passionate about taking therapy beyond the consulting room, sharing honest, supportive insights drawn from her personal and professional experience. She offers encouragement through her books, Instagram (@annamathur), online courses, in-person events and her podcast, *The Therapy Edit*, which has reached over four million downloads. Anna also works with corporate organizations to support mental wellbeing and regularly shares her thoughts in national media, including TV, radio and press.

The Good Decision Diary

Your Daily Guide to Making Better
Decisions, More of the Time

Anna Mathur

PENGUIN LIFE

AN IMPRINT OF

PENGUIN BOOKS

PENGUIN LIFE

UK | USA | Canada | Ireland | Australia
India | New Zealand | South Africa

Penguin Life is part of the Penguin Random House group of companies
whose addresses can be found at global.penguinrandomhouse.com

Penguin Random House UK,
One Embassy Gardens, 8 Viaduct Gardens, London SW11 7BW

penguin.co.uk

Penguin
Random House
UK

First published 2025
001

Set in 12/18pt TT Commons Classic
Typeset by Jouve (UK), Milton Keynes
Printed at Thomson Press India Ltd, New Delhi

The authorized representative in the EEA is Penguin Random House Ireland,
Morrison Chambers, 32 Nassau Street, Dublin D02 YH68

A CIP catalogue record for this book is available from the British Library

ISBN: 978-0-241-70722-7

Penguin Random House is committed to a sustainable future
for our business, our readers and our planet. This book is made from
Forest Stewardship Council® certified paper.

MIX
Paper | Supporting
responsible forestry
FSC® C018179

I dedicate this book to my husband, Tarun.

The best decision I ever made.

Contents

CONTENTS

CONTENTS

Introduction

If you're tired of breaking the promises you've made to
yourself, if your New Year's resolutions fall by the wayside
every January, if you always feel like you're failing to live
up to your own standards, this book is for you. We all want
to better ourselves in some way, to find ways to live a little
easier and happier. We seek more contentment, more
gratitude, that spring in our step. Yet we recognize that
there is a constant pull on our attention from the streams
of information that barrage every waking hour. We get
bombarded with contradictory chatter telling us the way
we're doing things is all wrong and offering a thousand
opinions on how to get it right. Is it any wonder we struggle
to make decisions?

Most of us know what we want to change, and where we
want to take ourselves. We want to nourish our bodies
more intentionally, we want to invest more time in the
relationships that mean the most to us, or we want to
end the habit of scrolling our way to sleep at night. And
all the information out there tells us change is do-able

as long as we apply enough drive and discipline. Yet in order to change, we face the challenge of shaking off old habits that we know don't serve us but are hell-bent on sticking around. The habits we form and the decisions we make undoubtedly shape our lives, and we know this. We recognize the power of our own decisions when we talk about turning points, sliding-doors moments and the butterfly effect, so why do we often find ourselves making decisions that keep us on a path we don't truly want to be on?

This isn't just about big decisions either. The small decisions slowly add up, gradually leading us further away from our bigger goals. Picking up our smartphones in the morning instead of our dumb-bells for the workout we said we'd do. Eating toast for dinner instead of using up the veg that's sitting untouched at the bottom of the fridge. This book is my attempt to share how I came to make better decisions, more of the time, and how you can too.

I'm Anna Mathur, a psychotherapist and a recovering all-or-nothing-er. I've spent my life trying to grow, shake off destructive habits, put an end to my sabotaging ways and soften my cruel inner dialogue. I would throw myself into new habits and ambitions with everything I had, confident

I could transform myself almost immediately. And then as soon as my new habits were challenged by an illness or a diary clash, they'd fall by the wayside. Nothing I started felt sustainable or flexible. In my mind I was either thriving or failing, and nothing in between.

I knew I wanted change, but I realized that the way I was setting goals and trying to form habits was just cueing me up for failure and self-criticism. Changing the way I made decisions helped me to find a new, sustainable and gentle way to grow. I've got a new kind of plan that you can't fail to keep and it's changing my life. I hope it's going to change yours too.

Finding a new way to grow

I invite you to find a new way to grow and change. A method that takes into account your humanness and acknowledges how hard it can be to break the destructive habits that seem to come as naturally as breathing. This new method recognizes what many do not: the nuances of everyday life. How a decision that is nurturing on one day might be sabotaging the next, depending on how you make that decision and how you feel about yourself. *The Good Decision Diary* will guide you towards knowing yourself well enough to be able to determine the difference between the two. This new method removes inflexible goals and aims, and finds you living more fully and contentedly instead, whatever that may look like for you in the different seasons of your life.

This isn't about becoming some flawless version of yourself who never makes a bad call. It's not about winning or succeeding, but developing good habits that will benefit you for the rest of your time on this earth. It's about ensuring that your inner voice is supporting your growth and not hindering it, nor waiting to pounce with a torrent of criticism should you make a decision that you regret. It's about getting to a place where you turn to yourself with kind enquiry rather than harsh criticism, where the motivation to make good decisions springs from a desire to care for yourself, rather than being driven by shame.

We are so aware, even if not consciously, that life is finite, that time is our most precious resource. Yet its disappearance is something no one can control. We feel the pressure of not making the most of our time, yet find ourselves wasting it as we live on autopilot, getting lost in our phones and our worries.

We fear making the wrong decision, looking back over our lives and wondering if we lived enough. So, we pledge to do, to grow, to reach, to push, to be the best we can be, to squeeze the last drops of juice out of the lemon of life, so that one day we might sit back and know we did it well. However, this bar of perfection is always out of reach. And guilt, shame and self-criticism lurk in that cavernous-looking gap between the life we feel we should be living and the reality of our ongoing bad habits. Despite our best intentions, we struggle to make the good decisions we know will help us live and love more fully.

So, is there something wrong with the goals we are reaching for, or is there something wrong with the way we are reaching for them? Is there something bad about the decisions we make, or is it the way we are approaching them and how we navigate the feelings that arise after we make them?

The Good Decision Diary is an interactive method to help you move towards your goals, free from feelings of failure or self-criticism. This book requires commitment – not huge commitment, but commitment all the same. When we want to establish a new way of approaching something, consistency is key. To make the most out of this book, find a quiet time and corner each day to give yourself the space you need and deserve.

As you progress through this book, you will be regularly invited to respond to guided prompts. Writing things down enables us to observe, put words to and externally process our thoughts.

How to Use
The Good
Decision Diary

My hope is that this book will take you five weeks to read, for no more than ten minutes per day. You may take longer than this – life gets in the way – but I encourage you to commit to following the book through in order for just thirty-five days. Taking the process step by step will open your eyes to a whole new way to approach decision-making. Not expecting perfection, but establishing a new method that will find you living more fully and in a manner reflective of your values.

The book consists of three sections:

Part One: (Days 1–7) REFLECTION

(5–10 minutes per day) Read at any time of day. In this section I have poured out the thoughts in my mind as I considered the decisions and actions in my own life, in the hope it will stir your own reflections. I share my own story and therapeutic thoughts over a week. I encourage you to read one chapter a day and let the words prompt thought and self-awareness. Spotting the patterns in your thoughts and behaviour is the first step to changing them. This self-reflection will set you up for turning inwards in Part Two.

Part Two: (Days 8–21) OBSERVATION

(5–7 minutes per day) This is your opportunity to arm yourself with all you need in order to begin the 'Change' part of the plan in Part Three. You will add a huge dose of humanness into your goals and plans, and cultivate an inner dialogue that will support you in making good decisions. I share two pages of thoughts on differing topics each day and the pages are dotted with journal prompts for you to respond to.

Part Three: (Days 22–35) CHANGE

(5–10 minutes a day) For fourteen days you will consider the decisions you have made each day, reflecting upon them in a non-judgemental way. You will learn and cement a tool or approach that you can use for the rest of your life. This will usher you on to grow in the way that's right for you, and at a pace in line with your level of resources and support.

Permission statement

While I hope this book will guide you towards incorporating more awareness into your goals and hopes, don't force yourself into the process to the detriment of your well-being in any way. This guide is here to enhance your life rather than hinder or overwhelm you.

So, if you need a break from the daily prompts or your mind is too full to add anything new, give yourself permission to pause. Nudge guilt aside, because you are not hindering your goal by giving yourself a break, but tending to your well-being . . . and isn't that ultimately what you're aiming for?

Part One

REFLECTION

────

For the first seven days of this *Good Decision Diary*,
I'm sharing my own experiences with you to prompt
your own reflections on how you speak to yourself, make
decisions and break habits. Let your eyes wander over the
words and allow your mind to wonder without judgement
or comparison. I encourage you to read a chapter a day.
If you already journal, then go ahead and journal, but I
won't be providing any journal guidance until next week,
so just use this time to consider where our experiences
meet and where they diverge.

Don't worry if you miss a day of reading, just pick it back
up when you feel able. There's no need to double-up on
reading two days at once to catch up; take it at your own
pace. Absorb and digest.

Day 1

Realizations in the Shower

As I stood in the shower one evening, I glanced down at my body under the cascade of water. 'I'm so good to you,' I whispered. 'And I'm so cruel.' Following this thought came a stream of echoes of the many promises I'd made myself over the years about my health: 'I'll do better tomorrow'; 'I'll start again on Monday'; 'On January the first, it's all going to change.'

And it's not just my health. I've made pledges, I've started journals, created checklists, devoured podcasts, downloaded apps, signed up to memberships, read ALL the books, sought allegiance with friends who share common goals to 'Let's do this together'. I've tried and I've tr ed to make better decisions consistently. And I've failed and fallen.

As a psychotherapist, I've found there's a common thread that weaves through the reasons people seek to embark on therapy: they want to change something in their lives, and they know that comes with making better decisions. They experience the slightly tormenting sensation that comes from making decisions, again and again, that don't align with their values or the goals they've set. They know what they want to do, what they need to do, yet time and time again they find themselves walking down the same familiar, well-trodden path of old habits and bad choices. I know that feeling. And I bet you do too.

So, I stood in the shower reflecting on the stark realization that despite all my efforts to try to do the 'right things', I often make decisions that sabotage me. I want to eat in a way that honours my body, yet I find myself bingeing, buckling up my seat belt on the sugar-high roller coaster, knowing that the crash will come as quickly as the remorse. I pledge to hold healthy boundaries, yet 'Sure, I'll take on that project' tumbles out of my mouth, swiftly followed by regret and resentment.

The battlefield

Cognitively, I know, and teach, that we humans are creatures of habit. I know that growth is a bumpy upwards wiggly line rather than a steep straight one drawn on a graph with a ruler. This isn't unique to individuals either. As a culture I notice that we are consistently tempted to opt for the quick fix that keeps our economy growing, while in the longer term these quick fixes leave our collective well-being challenged. We're living on a battlefield, fighting to thrive, while stronger forces – both internal and external – beckon us like sirens towards the rocks of self-sabotage and overwhelm.

I am the first to admit that I'm an 'all or nothing' person. I dive headlong into new habits, certain this is a fresh start defined by better decisions. I immerse myself in information, with verbal cheerleaders in the form of podcasts and audio books on 1.5 speed, piped through my headphones in the hopes I'll find my resolve. 'I'm not drinking alcohol any more,' I declare. Or 'I'm living in line with my menstrual cycle from this point onwards, until it comes to a halt.' 'I'm a runner now,' I think, lacing up my new trainers.

I've learned to recognize that I'm like a magpie to the shiny, hope-filled promises that come with well-picked soundbites and headlines: 'This might be the thing that will make life feel more straightforward, my head feel freer and my values feel easier to live out.' A fresh start feels fun and motivating, like I've got a clear plan and purpose. Onwards I storm in a haze of dopamine and drive.

The shame game

However, the high of the 'all' is soon followed by the shame-tinged crash of the 'nothing', as my overambitious plans fall by the wayside. I try to style it out and conclude, 'Well, it's all about balance, really, isn't it?' The thing is, if I'm totally honest, I'm not really interested in finding 'balance' when it comes to habits that sabotage me. I don't want 'balance' if it finds me riding high on pride one day as I've hit a goal and sinking into a spiral of regret the next. The highs never last long, and the regret tastes like bitter bile, corroding my self-trust and my well-being.

I struggle with balance. Perhaps you do too? I find it hard to know when to push on and when to slow down. I've exercised through bugs and bruises, tears and tiredness. I've been a slave to regimes that have started off feeling empowering, yet at points have felt harmful in my reluctance to give myself a break. Perhaps most importantly, I've struggled to recognize that point when the empowering decision has tipped into relentless self-punishment. I've copied magical morning routines that looked inspiring on social media, yet have sapped more energy than they've provided me with, leaving me frazzled and lacking sleep, wondering why the magic isn't magicking, or whether it's me that's broken.

I've used shame to rocket-launch myself into change after I've shoved sickening numbers of milk chocolate squares into my mouth on a Sunday night, going to bed wired with sugar and sleepless with guilt. Because tomorrow the only chocolate I'm 'allowed' is a square of excruciatingly bitter 100 per cent cocoa.

It's exhausting to live on a roller coaster of the best-set intentions, and then the crashes of guilt that inevitably follow. I'm a clever woman – I've written books upon books, my knowledge of human psychology is woven throughout my thoughts and shapes the lens through which I see the world – yet I keep doing the same thing over and over again. The high of intentions and promises, the hope that

PART ONE: REFLECTION

This time it WILL be different, and then the familiar crash of disappointment and shame as I find myself back in the rut I refuse to call 'home'. Albert Einstein is known to have said that 'Insanity is doing the same thing over and over again and expecting different results'. So then, I wonder, am I insane?

While shame can act as a rather effective catapult into change and submission to your new plan to make better decisions, I have learned from bitter experience that it is not an effective fuel for sustainable change. Shame chips away at self-worth. Consider the times you've used shame as a catapult; recall the vitriol, the disgust or disappointment the language of your self-talk was undoubtedly laced with. If you use this tone with a colleague or a child, they may well do as you ask out of fear, but their connection with you will have been harmed in the process. The same is true for your connection to yourself.

When I've relied on shame to be my driver for change, it's always there, lying in wait at the first or second hurdle I trip over for me to fall at its feet. Just as the addict needs bigger hits as the body becomes accustomed to a drug, I've needed bigger amounts of self-shame to get me up off my feet and trying harder. The shame gets more vicious as the cycle goes on.

I have a stark memory of a bootcamp workout I joined once, years ago. The personal trainer jeered and shouted at all of us. He kept adding repetitions on at the last second as my body was desperate to collapse into rest. I've never worked out so hard. It was like my internal dialogue had taken the human form of a shouting man. I never went back. As much as I was a glutton for shame-driven motivation, receiving it from myself was more than enough. Nobody is thriving when they're being screamed at. Especially not when the screaming is coming from inside.

A different kind of pledge

Back to the shower. As I stood there, I made yet another pledge to myself. But this one was different. It wasn't goal-orientated, nor was it pinned to any promise or outcome. This was a promise to seek well-being with full awareness of the state of my human fallibility.

It was this: *Make good decisions, more of the time.* That was all. Not *all* of the time. I gently nudged myself away from all-or-nothing, and accepted the possibility of more good choices in place of unrealistic promises of perfection. I pledged to begin to notice the crossroads of decision that I encountered each day, the big and the small, the life-altering ones and the ones I'd usually autopilot my way through, and face them all with intention. Some decisions are so insignificant that my brain barely registers them as decisions (do I defrost the blueberries or raspberries?), and some are so deeply ingrained that I don't yet realize I am even making a decision.

But in those moments when I *was* aware I faced a choice in how to act or think, I pledged to ask myself whether I wished to make a decision that would help, halt or hinder my growth. It felt starkly simple.

Obviously, if it were that simple, I wouldn't be writing a whole book about it, would I? I'd write an article, a blog or a social media post, throw it out there and call it a day. But I'd be doing this transformation a huge injustice if I summed it up in just a fridge-magnet-style affirmation. I'd be overlooking the journey I went on from that first decision. And I'd be skimming over the complexity of the human mind when it comes to decision-making, the stories we carry, the narratives we are led by and the depth of those reasons why we sometimes choose, against all our best intentions, to take the road that leads to regret.

The nuances at the crossroads

If I were to leave you with the simple request to 'Make better decisions more of the time, choosing the option that will help your growth rather than halt or hinder it', I'd be sidestepping the fact that the very same action could help you one day and sabotage you the next.

For example, I value an early morning. With three young children, sometimes that quiet hour before they get up is a gift. I'll set an alarm and enjoy a short time of journalling, maybe some yoga or a workout, and almost certainly a coffee before the chaos begins. This hour nurtures me, sets me up, resources me before I butter bagels, pack lunches and tend to tantrums. And yet some days the alarm goes off and everything in me wants to turn over and slide back into my dream.

I've really had to get to know myself in order to understand when to turn off that alarm and succumb, guilt-free, to those extra moments of needed rest, and when to summon my inner parent to straight-talk myself out of bed and into my workout leggings. Sometimes to turn over is to sabotage; sometimes it's an act of nurturing my well-being. We need the wisdom to know the difference, and that's what you'll have by the end of *The Good Decision Diary*.

If I were to reduce this shower-prompted 'Make more good decisions' tip into nothing more than a shareable social media square, I'd be missing out the importance of knowing how the language we use in the secret place of our minds has the power to drive us towards growth or despair. How you speak to yourself matters deeply.

Questioning the commentary

That constant commentary that plays through your mind like a radio you can't turn off or down is the most important soundtrack you'll ever hear. How you speak to yourself matters. The tone that soundtrack takes, the words and language used when you drop the butter on the floor ('You idiot'), double-book your friend ('What's wrong with me?'), or arrive late to the meeting ('Everyone thinks I'm disorganized'), have the power to dictate the course of your life, let alone your day.

Your inner dialogue can be the bully that tempts you in the face of decisions and torments you in the aftermath. Or it can be the supportive parent figure who knows what's right for you and encourages you to make decisions based upon needs rather than impulsive desire. A friend who is there for you, without judgement, when it all seems to go pear-shaped. And the most incredible thing is that just as your inner dialogue was formed over time, so it can be reshaped.

My aim in this book is to explore the importance of taking an enquiring stance as you face and make decisions, rather than a judgemental one.

When I make a decision that I perceive as 'wrong' or 'bad' (sometimes only seconds later, sometimes even as I'm consciously making the decision that isn't in alignment with my hopes, values or goals), I can instantly berate myself. Standing at the coffee machine with already shaking hands and pumping adrenaline, I know two cups is enough for me. I know if I make another coffee my heart will be racing for the next hour, and I'll be highly strung and snappy throughout the already adrenaline-fuelled rush hour of my day, but still I press the button to fill my cup yet again. My judgemental voice kicks in as quickly as the first drip of coffee splashes into the mug: 'You're ridiculous. You knew that wasn't the right thing to do. Why are you so weak? Why can't you stick to anything?' When I take this judgemental stance, it's like my inner child shuts down, cowers and promises to do better next time in order to placate the anger. There is no reflection, just shame and a pledge to try harder. I drink the hot coffee guiltily, at double speed, like the shoplifter who gulps down the stolen drink as security staff come running.

However, when I choose to take a more enquiring stance with myself, that inner child becomes more open to conversation. 'I wonder why you went for that third coffee? Did it seem impossible to make the decision that deep down you wanted to make? How were you feeling as you faced that decision?' Asking questions without judgement uncovers answers and prompts new realizations. I conclude that I was tired, stressed and fed up in that moment. I was guilt-filled for snapping at my partner and chose to sabotage myself as a sort of penance. Compassion edges into me in place of shame: 'You might feel guilty for the way you snapped, but that is no reason to sabotage. Why don't you text him to apologize and face the guilt instead of inhaling more caffeine?'

Onwards

That shower of mine only lasted a couple of minutes, yet when I look back, it prompted such a shift in how I understand growth, habits and decision-making. As you move through your day today, perhaps you too will begin to notice the language you use in the quiet of your mind. Consider what part shame or compassion play as you dance around decisions. Let my musings settle and see what arises for you.

Day 2

The World's Way

Reflecting on all the different ways I have navigated the decisions that line my path towards my goals, I realize I have repeatedly fallen into the same trap. No matter what decision I am making, or what goal I am pursuing, my mistake has been to believe that there must be one way that works, one discipline, plan, map to follow that will find me falling in line with my own values once and for all.

Nothing has ever worked for me for long, and perhaps that isn't because I haven't found the 'right way', but because there is no true 'right way'. If there were, we'd know about it by now, wouldn't we? The one true guide to achieving optimal well-being and making good decisions with a 100 per cent success rate would be the meteorite to obliterate all other self-help guides ever written. But the uncomfortable truth is that there is no one guide and no single way to make good, lasting change. Life is more nuanced, bumpy, changeable and messy than that. And knowing this is encouraging, because it means there are many paths up the mountain – you just have to find the one that works for you.

Broken mantras

When we seek to make better decisions in any area of our life, we seek motivating mantras to cheerlead us on our way, to hang on to in times of temptation. They are all variations on 'do better, reach higher, push harder, you can do this, don't give up, better things are ahead, be strong'. Oftentimes they do the trick, injecting us with a burst of intention. But what about when these same mantras fail us?

There are times when repeating the encouragement 'You've got this' serves me well. When I sit down at my laptop to see a newly opened blank document waiting for 60,000 words to be written, 'You've got this, Anna' feels like a battle cry as I dive right in and recall previous occasions when I've found the words flowing out of me and my fingers flying across the keys of my laptop. Yet there are times when that same encouragement feels like a suffocating expectation, calling upon resources that I do not have to reach a goal I cannot humanly stretch to. 'You've got this' feels almost cruel when I'm facing that same blank document on a day when, for example, I'm processing a friend's cancer diagnosis.

Mantras and encouragements can pick us up and spur us on to take first steps and get back on the path of good decisions. But without taking into account our humanness and ever-changing resources, the same mantra can feel demoralizing and judgemental.

Five steps to a healthier you

I am drawn to promises and plans like a moth to a flame. Growth simplified, failsafe, tried and tested. I have followed many step-by-step plans to the letter, and then my all-or-nothing mentality finds me shutting the book and placing it on the shelves with the others to gather dust as soon as my craving, tiredness or short attention span win over. There's no way I could let a book sit, winking accusingly at me, from my bedside table, a reminder of yet another failure to adhere to simple steps. I take steps all the time as I move from one place to another, so why can't I take these?

If I truly believed that a better life wasn't possible, and that all roads led to nowhere, I'd never try. I recall the endless nights of my second child's sleeplessness. Unbeknownst to me, he had an undiagnosed condition which was affecting his sleep. Night after night, I'd hold on to the hope that maybe 'tonight will be the night we sleep'. It's almost heartbreaking when I reflect back on how tightly I held on to that hope. It was this hope that prevented me from seeking the support I (and he) needed. Instead, I believed it was something I was somehow doing wrong. When we blame ourselves for what seems like relentless failure, we are less able to seek out what it is that we need in order to thrive. Sometimes that means asking for help.

The blame I placed on myself for never being able to stick to a new routine or habit for long prevented me from observing myself and enquiring with kindness why this pattern was repeating. I thought perhaps it was because I'd not found the right plan, or not tried hard enough, rather than realizing that my body was craving more nutrients, or I wasn't sleeping well enough to summon the energy to journal for as long as the plan dictated. Or perhaps I was sabotaging my own growth due to low self-esteem and a subconscious disbelief that I was deserving of good things. I wanted to place better boundaries around my relationships and to strengthen my voice to find a healthy 'no', as the books said, yet if deep down I struggled with people feeling disappointed in me, or misunderstanding me, no wonder it felt like a battle. Holding healthier boundaries meant I'd be more likely to face disappointment or misunderstanding from others, and that felt intolerable. Failure was easier to handle, as the only person I was letting down was myself.

With reflection, I believe I will always be drawn towards the steps and the plans, the podcasts and the books brimming with hope and promise. But since my shower moment I have started to consume them through the lens of my own fallible, exhaustible humanness. I will hold these shiny promises in open hands and say 'This looks interesting' rather than grasping them with a white-knuckle grip as if for dear life.

It's not easy, when we're constantly tempted by new things, to remember that nothing is ever as it seems. When we're sold the well-watered plant, we picture it in a particular spot in our home, believing it will be the cherry on the cake for the newly decorated room. In the fantasy, we forget the fact that our plant won't look quite the same when we stick it on a shelf and haphazardly water it. Or the holiday that looks as good on the website as it appears in our daydreams, until we get there and there are the usual delays at the baggage carousel, the overcrowded pool and the slivers of burnt skin that escaped the daubing of sunscreen. The fantasy is wonderful until you add an inescapable dose of reality.

We know what you need

I used to love those colourful flow charts in magazines that you tracked down with your finger to determine the best type of boyfriend for your personality. I liked the questionnaires we'd fill in on the clunky school computers that would spit out a handful of job recommendations. From a young age, we've been provided with strong ideas and nudges towards what we should reach for or desire. Even *in utero* we are measured against graphs, our growth projections tracked, our heights estimated. We are barely verbal before we realize we're being ushered towards milestones, targets and grades.

Many of these targets are rooted in necessity, I guess, the desire to measure against averages to determine whether we'd benefit from intervention or support. But I think what happened for me, and perhaps you, was that we learned from infancy to look outside of ourselves to be told what we should be reaching for, and how. And, of course, it's okay to take advice and encouragement from people who know more, or who have age and wisdom on their side.

However, I don't think I've been taught well enough, alongside all the advice, that my gut sense matters. That there's a little voice inside of me that has wisdom. It might not have all the knowledge that others do, but it knows *me*. That voice has a powerful sensitivity to the inside story of who I am. The world may tell me what I should want, but it's my gut sense that knows what I truly need. The plans will tell me to follow their protocol, but it's my gut sense that whispers whether it's too much for that day. The advice of others will tell me where to place boundaries and when to relax them, but it's my gut sense that whispers 'This isn't okay for me'.

The more we take every goal-, life- or habit-themed piece of advice at face value, the more we end up suppressing that gut sense. Oh, the times I've found myself questioning why I struggle to maintain or conform to something that seems so right, before discovering that it's just not right for *me*. Be it in that moment, that day, that season of my life, or . . . at all. And that's not a failing of any sort, it's just a result of highly individual humans offering guidance to highly individual humans. Even the guidance in this very book might not be for you. While I hope you may draw inspiration and encouragement from these pages, nobody can be for everyone.

Putting aside perfect

The other thing I've had to address when it comes to bringing my daily decisions more in line with my hopes and values is the fact that perfection is a myth sold to keep us striving, small and buying stuff. It's much more effective for our culture and economy when we are kept small, as we are less likely to pipe up about issues that stir us, or to disrupt the status quo. And it's much easier to sell us solutions. When we feel shame, we think that we are the problem in the pursuit of 'getting life right'. When we realize that we are inherently flawed and we will never reach the rightness we have been taught to stretch for, we can find our voices, grow in confidence and take our space imperfectly, making the most of the circumstances we find ourselves in.

When I worked in an advertising agency in my early twenties, I'd beat myself up viciously for any detail I overlooked. Any feedback with the remotest bit of criticism and I'd do everything I could to put it right and appease. I'd say 'yes' to every request regardless of my resources and would strive publicly while burning out in private, harbouring secret resentment at those who'd asked of me. However, since finding a healthier way to grow, I hold boundaries, I say 'no' when I need to, I ask for support as well as giving it. I'm no longer 'easy-breezy, I'll be whoever you want me to be'; I value myself as much as I value others. I no longer contort and shrink myself but ask for the same respect I offer others.

So yes, once we begin to realize that so many of the goals we set ourselves are unrealistic ambitions set by perfectionism, we adjust them. And as well as growing, we begin to take up more space in our own lives; we feel empowered to make more good decisions. It's hard and it's wonderful.

We can so easily see growth through the lens of perfection, that smooth, upwards line on a graph devoid of kinks and smudges. I found myself imagining it was possible to grow like that. Would I end up brilliantly self-aware, with perfect habits and a routine that put anyone to shame? How many friends would I have around me at that point, when every utterance that tumbled out of my mouth was word-perfect and woven with wisdom? Most importantly, would this steep line of growth ever stop? Would I die before I reached 'fully grown'? The more I pondered this, the more ridiculous it seemed.

If you have been pulled into the seductive belief that personal growth should have an ever-upwards trajectory, I'll share with you a metaphor that came to me, which I conjure up whenever I find myself leaning towards perfectionism as I face decisions, or set goals, hopes and intentions.

Consider a healthy tree growing sturdily, housing birds in nests. It is strong, it is well, it is thriving. Yet it still has a limited lifespan, a few aphid-eaten leaves and areas of scarred bark. The trunk tells stories of branches ripped off by storms, one branch bears apples, the other looks like it has quite given up. There is no perfection, far from it, yet the picture of the tree as a whole is of strength and life. In my mind, this tree is me. Flawed and thriving.

The roots underground span out. Imagine tracing them with your eyes. For me, these are the growth lines that signify all the attempts, the decisions I've made, the roads of growth I've gone down. Some branch off, forming separate veins, reaching out into fertile soil. Some roots are thin and short; some stop abruptly as they've grown up against the face of a hard rock; others have snaked their way around these obstacles. All of this trying, halting, giving up, trying something else, persevering, establishing habits and hopes, forms each and every root.

We might look at this tangle of roots just as we look over our attempts and failings to make good decisions, to form habits and hold hopes. We see the failures, the little mini deaths of roots that have shrivelled. We might look at them and see the ones that have grown off-piste, finding their own way, or the ones that stopped growing the second they hit the obstacles in their pebble-strewn path. However, I want to draw your attention back to the tree, back to the you that exists right now. Each of those roots, no matter how far or deep they grew, or for however long, all contributed to the growth of the tree that sits above them.

As I've let my mind ruminate over this metaphor, I've found that compassion has blossomed for everything

I've experienced. Instead of seeing all my dusty books, my half-consumed podcasts, my semi-filled journals as failures, I can see how they have all contributed to where I am today. I might not have finished all of these things, but I'll never be a finished product myself, and neither will you.

Day 3

Hitting the Reset Button

I love a reset button. I remember office days when a member of the tech team would come over and fix all our computer problems with a simple hit of the reset button. We hadn't tried that. We didn't think it would be that simple. Trying to recreate this feeling, I've grabbed a whole new journal from the shelf, despite the fact that my current one still boasts so many blank pages. I want to feel new, I want to wipe the slate clean, to start afresh, to begin a different story. It reminds me of the frustration that would roll over me as I messed up a page of my school book and sought to hide it with clots of white corrector.

When it comes to making good decisions, there is no reset button. We cannot wipe sabotaging decisions, hurtful words or steamrollered boundaries out of our history. We cannot undo the fact that we chose to walk down paths that hindered us, scared us, scarred us. We cannot hit reset on relationships. We can forgive ourselves and others, we can find new ways, form new paths, but we cannot reset entirely. Everything we do and have done comes with a cost and a consequence. Just like those tree roots that halt or reroute, our decisions can't ungrow and regrow in a better way. Even so, they all contribute, in time, to the strength and health of the tree despite how small or stunted they are.

Oh, the roads of destruction I've travelled down. The relationships I've wholeheartedly invested in that have left me feeling untrusting and insecure. The gruelling kilometres I've forced myself to run, despite my body screaming 'no', in order to tick a box of a plan or a calorie-burning goal. I've worn myself out, harmed myself from the inside out. Over the years, I've probably done lasting damage with some of the harmful habits I've pursued, the sabotaging decisions I've made, the ruts I've struggled to reach my way out of and the misplaced hopes I've held.

But, instead of beating myself up, I have learned to see these decisions as the rich tangle of roots that make up the tree that I am today. The slightly weather-beaten, nest-bearing, insect-nibbled tree that stands tall and strong amidst the others around me. I have learned that this is the only way I'll ever truly be, and that I am worthwhile and of value like this regardless of my flaws and broken bits. Although I now accept I'll never reach all of my well-intended goals, I still believe it's worth pursuing wellness and growth. Despite the failings and floundering, I am still growing, learning and finding new ways to thrive. And that's surely worth all the stop–starts and plans that fall by the wayside. The game-changer for me is accepting and expecting the obstacles and dead ends of the journey, rather than shaming myself for them.

But I haven't wholly let go of the reset button. Instead, I've adapted it. I no longer give in to the temptation to grab the fresh journal from the shelf, or tear out pages after I've flicked back to see missed dates and sloppily scrawled entries. I hit the reset button *exactly where I am.* I give myself permission to start afresh from the point that I find myself at. And the good thing about this reset button? You can hit it endless times. Sometimes I hit it multiple times a day, or even an hour. I know I can hit reset as often as I need. It's permission to start again from where I find myself.

The red 'guilt' flag

When I choose to do something that I really know isn't ideal for me, I feel guilt. Now, guilt generally serves a great purpose for me and I've learned to befriend it and listen to it. In my mind I see guilt as this small red flag that pops out, quite like the little orange-red trafficators that used to pop out on old cars to signal which way they were turning. These little trafficators aren't aggressive, blaring alarms, and they don't give out an unavoidably dazzling, strobing glare that will stun your sight. No, they're just pointing something out to you.

Guilt is a gentle alert, a feeling that rises up within my core, a small sense of dis-ease that invites me to pay attention and act somehow. Maybe it prompts me to apologize to someone, to hold a boundary, to seek support or clarity. Guilt invites me to turn towards it.

Perhaps I feel guilty because I responded rudely to someone in the car beside me who nearly cut me up. They did wrong, intentionally or unintentionally, yet it didn't warrant rudeness. As I shouted through the window, I felt guilt. That guilt alerted me to the fact that I'd acted out of alignment with my values, hopes and intentions. It wasn't a persecutory 'Why would you do that?' or a shaming 'What is wrong with you?', it was a factual alert of 'Oh, that response didn't feel right for you, did it, Anna?'

So, as I turn towards that popped-up flag, I can engage an enquiring mind and ask myself 'What happened there?' I conclude that I'm grumpy and tired, and while I'd apologize to the other driver if I could, I won't get that opportunity. So how might I refuel, rest or resource myself so that if another irritation occurs today, I might be able to respond differently?

When guilt malfunctions

Sometimes guilt stems from a destructive internal narrative, so listen to it carefully to ensure it's not prompting unnecessary shame. Sometimes that little guilt flag pops up and demands my attention, yet when I turn towards it and see what triggered it, it's actually a malfunction. Let's continue with the car theme. Sometimes, one of the car alarms goes off in the homes around where we live. We look out of the window to see that perhaps it was triggered by a kid careering into it with a scooter, or perhaps it just malfunctioned. The car's security wasn't truly at threat, but for a moment there, be it from a strong gust of wind or an excitable child that hadn't yet mastered the scooter brake, the system perceived threat.

In the same way, sometimes I turn towards my feeling of guilt and see that actually it has malfunctioned, much like the car alarm. I feel the guilt, the dis-ease that something I've done or said is out of line with a value, goal or hope I hold, and I discover that actually it's my deepest narrative of perfectionism that triggered it: 'I made a not-so-great decision, therefore I failed. GUILT, GUILT.' As I turn towards this guilt with enquiry, I recognize that I'm viewing growth through my perfectionistic lens. I didn't email my colleague back and I feel guilt. Yet I recognize that I've been leaning into a people-pleasing, fear-fuelled narrative that if I don't get back to people really quickly, they will be displeased with me.

In truth, I recognize I've had a lot on my plate and I'm sure that colleague can withstand a delay in response. And, in fact, my cognitive mind knows that this cultural expectation of immediacy isn't really serving us, but fuelling burnout. As I go through that short process of gentle self-enquiry, I can see that my guilt flag popped up unnecessarily. I haven't done anything 'wrong' per se.

So I can choose to release it. I imagine flicking the flag back down into its resting place and hitting the reset button.

When it goes unaddressed, guilt can landslide into shame. Guilt says 'It wasn't ideal to make that decision, let's talk about it'. Shame says 'You've messed up again, you might as well give up now'. Simply put, guilt says 'That failed', and shame turns it into a statement about the entirety of who you are and says '*You* are the failure'. Shame leaves us feeling deeply flawed, believing that perhaps we might be broken beyond repair. And when we lean into shame, we might ask 'What's even the point of trying again?', believing that if we seek support or accountability, someone may find us a lost cause. No one is a lost cause – there is always hope.

Not carrying shame from one moment to the next

For me, 'hitting reset' when it comes to making conscious decisions and forming nurturing habits is all about ensuring that I don't carry the guilt and shame from one moment or decision into the next. When we approach growth and good decision-making with this all-or-nothing mentality, we can feel like we've fallen off the path we so wanted to stay on, as if it's a tightrope and a single misstep has us tumbling so far down into the crevasse below that there's no point in even attempting to remount.

So, what do we do? We can find ourselves thinking 'Sod it, I've fallen now, I might as well write today off and restart tomorrow'. We overlook the opportunity to set ourselves back on the path that best serves us and rely on that shame to catapult us into starting again tomorrow, or at some other point in the future. We end up essentially giving ourselves permission to sabotage further, delaying the opportunity to nurture ourselves.

It strikes me that I wouldn't take this stance in certain situations. I wouldn't think: 'Oh man, I yelled at my kid when I've been really trying to work on responding calmly. Scrap that, I'll just scream at them all day now and start again with the calm responses tomorrow.' Or 'That project I finished for my colleague was below par. Oh well, I'll drop my standards for the rest of the week and start afresh on Monday.'

The more we shame ourselves for falling off any wagon we've climbed upon, the longer we'll spend rolling around in the dusty consequences, like the alcoholic who takes a sip of wine and then thinks 'Well, I've messed up now, might as well drink the bar dry'. One sip, one slip, one moment of veering off course has some consequence, but when we choose to keep running in the direction that conflicts with our values and hopes, that's a bigger decision that comes with a bigger set of consequences.

The more I choose to respond to myself with an enquiring mind, the less fatalistic and bullying I am towards myself. And the more likely I am to recognize that I can decide to do things differently the next time. This isn't about overlooking consequences or denying that I made a hindering decision. No, this isn't about enforced amnesia that says 'Oh well, I'll forget that happened'. It's a decision not to shame myself in a way that will increase my chances of making the same decision again. Choosing to reset says 'That moment didn't go well, here's a fresh opportunity to make a different decision'.

Taking this stance means we're more likely to get back on the wagon or pursue the nurturing option next time we're faced with a decision, rather than thinking 'Well, I've broken it now'. It's like that tree root, and how it seeks a new pathway, instead of thinking 'Sod it, I'll stop growing, then' when it hits a pebble in the soil.

Don't hold off good things – health, joy, rest, connections and wellness – for another day, another month or even another year. Keep writing the journal despite the scruffy scrawling and crossing-out in the paragraph above. Keep making the decision to nurture yourself despite the fact that the last decision you made found you storming resolutely into sabotage. As you do this, you're growing *your* way.

Day 4

Deciding Not to Go It Alone

I am deeply privileged to have had many lovely and supportive relationships over the years. Yet for most of my life, I have felt as if there was a one-way, impermeable forcefield around me. I could give support out, but I couldn't let support in. I could offer supportive words, time, therapy, love, resources, but the forcefield around me blocked those same offerings from others. They would offer me support, kind words, comfort and the opportunity to be vulnerable, yet it fell at my feet and I gazed down at it, thinking, 'That was nice, but it's not for me.' Sometimes I'd even see their kind offers of support and wish deeply that I could accept them, yet I plastered on a smile and proclaimed 'I'm fine, how are you?' or 'That's so kind but I'm good, thanks'.

I often wonder if my desire to become a therapist was to professionalize my need to help others in order to earn my validity and place in this world: 'Oh, don't worry about me, let's talk about you.' This forcefield kept me feeling useful and secured my sense of identity as 'the helper'. Yet it also meant that I was my own go-to. In time, the life experiences racked up, bouts of depression rolled over me, internal challenges began to impact my external world and the 'strong independent woman' battle cry of 'I've got this' began to weaken. The smile I wore like a shield, that statement of 'Nothing to see here, it's all under control', cracked at the edges.

I began seeing a therapist as a requirement of my psychotherapy training. For me, at first, it was a tick-box exercise. I decided I'd play the role of the perfect client, while knowing there was nobody better to detangle and comb my thoughts into order than me. I'd sit neatly in the chair talking just enough to fill the silence, but believing I didn't need to be there.

I didn't need to talk about my disordered eating or overexercising, my trauma or the toxic dynamics in a close relationship because I was 'on it'. I was fixing myself. I knew why these coping mechanisms and these habits had woven seemingly inextricably into my life and mind, and I was in the process of straightening myself out. I would get there in the end. Me, myself and I.

I'd share small insights into my inner world, quickly followed by my own analysis of it and the steps I was taking to address it. 'You don't leave any room for me,' my therapist challenged. I didn't leave cracks wide enough for anyone to get inside and nurture the broken parts of me. I was fully capable of doing that myself, while taking care of everyone else's cracks too.

The learning curve

I was like a heart surgeon treating my own heart condition, shunning all potentially helpful advice from experienced colleagues because 'I know best for me'. It's all just about do-able and survivable until support has been overlooked for so long that open-heart surgery has to be the next step. Trust me, I tried that one too. If I could have done my own surgery, I would have. I was clambering through life refusing to lean on any of the shoulders offered to me.

Finally, the arm that had resolutely held the flag proclaiming 'I've got this' bowed, shook and ached. The ruts of the habits that were harming me were so deep that I kept slipping back into them at every crossroads of decision. I didn't have the energy to choose otherwise. It was hard to opt for decisions that would be helpful and nurturing when sabotage and chaos had become my familiar home. I was too tired to find newness, and shame had eroded the belief that I was truly deserving of the joy, life and vibrancy that other decisions held.

I hit a rock bottom of sorts. It wasn't found in the dregs of a bottle or a medical diagnosis, it was found in the tears that could no longer be held back and the red eyes that could no longer be camouflaged by yet another layer of make-up. It was found in a wave of fear and acknowledgement that as much as 'I've got this' had become my identity, finally admitting 'I've not got this' was the necessary key to unlock me from the jail of my suffocating self-sufficiency.

I need people. I had protected myself from this realization, this truth, this fact of my own humanness, for too long. Being the surgeon to my own heart had not kept me safe, nor had it kept others happy. They had seen a need they weren't allowed to meet. I had seen them halt at my forcefield; I wanted to let them in but didn't know how to switch it off. The truth of needing others to support me, to be kind to me, hear me, walk beside me through life's fires, at first felt like a failure of sorts. Being helped wasn't a role I liked to play, but I realized it was an essential part of being a content human.

Since then, there have been many times I've stood at the crossroads of decisions and felt the pull to continue down the well-trodden road of sabotage. And don't get me wrong, it's a road I continue to walk down on the regular. But not as often as I used to: now I can turn to my right or my left (really my phone) and know that people are standing beside me, willing me and cheering me on. The path of 'helpful' decisions is becoming more worn and well trodden under my feet and easier to stay on. The metaphorical tree is becoming taller and sturdier and, what's more, I now love that I am in a forest full of trees, with each one providing shelter, shade and nourishment for the other.

Don't go alone on the walk

These days, when wanting to stretch or grow, to make more good decisions, address habits or expand on goals,

I don't just devour information and trust on all that I've got inside of me to carry me through. No, I look around to see who is already walking a similar journey alongside me, or who might be willing to walk in step with me and offer accountability.

We humans are pack animals. We are safer when we journey together. Yet circumstances in life can find us hurt or our needs unmet and overlooked. We might decide that actually we'll avoid further pain if we go the rest of the way alone. We may well avoid the pain of being hurt by others when we put up the forcefield, but we also avoid opportunities for support, connection and wisdom, all of which are deep needs despite how hard we might try to manage alone.

We will be misunderstood, overlooked and harmed by others as we move through life. For we all have our blind spots, our toxic traits, and we all view each other through lenses scratched by life's experiences. This is yet another of life's human inevitabilities. Some people may not support me well, but it doesn't mean that nobody will. I've learned to not take it too deeply to heart if someone isn't able to say the right thing or see the part of me I want to share with them with the clarity I yearn for them to. Perhaps they don't have the capacity or insight to walk in step alongside me, or the insight to know how to sit with me wholeheartedly to hear the story of my soul. Perhaps my truth touches a truth of their own they're not willing to see. And that has to be okay, otherwise I'll choose to haul up the drawbridge. And it's lonely behind the drawbridge. If I want to make good change and make more of those nurturing decisions at the crossroads I find myself at, then I need to have others around me. We all do.

Look high and low, but make sure you look

As a mother, I have many times stumbled upon the trope 'motherhood takes a village'. As a therapist I believe that life itself takes a village. Yet there were times when I've looked around and wondered where on earth that village was. I have realized that the village is there, it's just that sometimes we have to look harder, sometimes we have to get creative, sometimes we need to hunt down the strangers and the communities who understand the nuances of our challenges. Online, offline, groups, individuals, movements or momentary connections, wherever they may be, if you're wondering where the village is, take time to find those people.

Social media is a double-edged sword, and it cuts sharply when you fall upon the wrong edge, yet we often find ourselves returning because we can discover even the most niche experiences reflected in the stories there, if we look hard enough. Sleepless with a screaming baby, I scrolled Facebook pages to find one full of mothers sleepless with screaming babies. Amidst the advice, I felt deeply seen by the vulnerable openness of hope and despair. With an autistic son, I have found deep connection with strangers in unexpected places who, with a simple glance, have communicated more understanding and compassion than I thought anyone could fit into the space of a single second. Knowing we're not alone spurs us on to keep taking the path that nurtures, because shame or assumptions of our own brokenness ebb away that little bit more when we realize we're part of a collective experience.

Our culture praises furious self-sufficiency, and often our identity can rest upon the outcomes of the things we plough our energy into. Other cultures do not work in this way, but tend towards the collective communities we have been edging away from over the generations. We all have our own reasons for wanting to fly the flag of 'I've got this'. My own likely stem from growing up around loss and subsequent grief. I lost my sister to cancer as a child and was surrounded by those processing their grief. I didn't want to add to the pain or trauma around me, so I internalized a lot of my feelings, choosing not to share them with my parents and caregivers but to nudge them deep down inside with a pledge to be a 'good girl'.

I often find my mind musing on the cavepeople who wouldn't have fared at all well if they had resolutely chosen to assume each and every role themselves: 'I stoke the fire and I hunt the food. I also stand on watch for predators while I tend to the land. I do it all so that I can revel in the glory of my own survival.' They wouldn't have survived for long.

As someone who has been self-employed for many years, I have struggled to hand over roles in order to continue doing what I am good at. I remember one year shedding tears as I watched videos and read articles to help me do something technical and web-based that was far out of my comfort zone. It has been hard at points to relinquish control and let others far more skilled than me step into roles that I found difficult, but letting go of those responsibilities has meant that I can focus and grow in a way that makes my business sustainable. I would hand over passwords and then change them in a panic, leaving someone confused and locked out of being able to do a job that I was paying them to do.

It has taken time, but these days I recognize how I need the skills and input of others in order to survive in a work context, just as I need others in my life in order to make good decisions more often that help me thrive mentally and physically. Goodness knows, I've grappled with that too. I've felt the vulnerability hangover as I've shared insights into the depths of my challenges with mental health, and the relief that comes when I realize that I really am stronger when I lean on others. It's a lesson I've had to learn over and over again, and probably always will in different ways as hidden layers of my long-standing self-sufficiency are revealed through life's inevitable challenges and knocks.

We tend to fear that our openness and vulnerability will push others away. In truth, I've learned both personally and through my role as a therapist that it's vulnerability which connects us with others. When I consider how it feels as others share their inner thoughts with me, I recognize a sense of immense privilege and connection. I take comfort from that thought when I take steps of vulnerability with others, and like any muscle, the ability to do so with less shame and fear has strengthened over time for me, as it will for you too. Not everyone will be able to give you what you need, say the right words or walk alongside you in your challenges, but the right people will. Seek them out.

Day 5

Stop Playing the 'When/Then' Game

When I've ticked off everything on my to-do list, *then* I'll finally rest. When I've hit my fitness goal, *then* I'll finally accept my body. When I achieve the promotion I have been working towards, *then* I'll finally get to wave goodbye to a feeling of imposterism. I have been almost a thus-far lifelong player of the 'when/then' game.

But as I've begun to live life with more awareness of its limitations as well as my own, I've realized that the 'when/then' game has left me holding back from some of life's best bits. I've held back from rest, joy, a glow of pride at my achievements. I've held back from giving my body the time, attention and support it deserves.

The fact of the matter is, I'm going to die. I don't say that in a defeatist way, but in a manner that makes me feel empowered and liberated from the relentless to-do lists, aims and goals of daily life. It's an attitude that helps me not to hold back on some of the things I need and yearn for until I've reached some fictitious end goal. Stuff needs to get done, habits benefit from being challenged, goals are great to set, intentions are wonderful to ponder. Yet it is a great and deep loss to forget that this one life is for the living along the way.

The uncomfortable truth

Too often do we hear of lives ended cruelly short. And the uncomfortable truth is that, regardless of how many plans we make and intentions we set, our life too could end at any moment. There is nobody in this world who lives outside of this predicament, so instead of letting it throw a petrol bomb upon your anxiety, let it nurture a shoot of liberation. I'll plan, I'll write to-do lists, I'll set intentions and move towards goals, but I will not hold back from truly living along the way. In fact, I will seek ways to make my life feel even more meaningful.

These days I remind myself to wear the clothes that make me happy regardless of whether someone might deem them a little 'much' for a Monday morning. I'm going to squirt my dusty bottle of fancy bubble bath liberally into the tub. What was I saving it for anyway? A special day? Despite the mundanity of the day at hand, I seek to remind myself that it is special because I am breathing, I can see the tops of the trees that will continue to grow long after I am gone, I can speak to family members who I love, I can make decisions that will nurture my body and mind so that I can live as fully as I can for the years I'm alive, however many they may be.

There will most likely be a to-do list of sorts with my name upon it until the day I die. Whether it's to unstack the dishwasher, pay the bills or arrange to see a loved one, life will never stop providing me with things to do. The list is endless, but my resources are not. The potential of things to be done is never-ending, but my life certainly is. As I make plans and set goals, I try to consider what hinges upon them coming to fruition. If it is pleasure, or a sense of accomplishment, or a rest, how can I embrace some of those things along the way?

As a therapist I have sat with so many people who have felt deep disillusionment at finally reaching their goal and discovering that they didn't experience the elation or sense of fulfilment they'd hoped they would. We all want that sense of being able to exhale and look at the view of how far we've fought and climbed, but what often happens is that we turn to see there is another hidden peak to the mountain, there is further to reach and strive. There will always be somewhere else to grow and go, and an infinite number of resources to guide you there. We will never feel like we've done all the growing we need to do, I don't think. To believe that we can is yet another fantasy we so often buy into that keeps us holding back from diving into life where we are.

So many of us reach for the 'more' that is dangled in front of us, wrapped up in shiny paper that promises us, if we work hard enough, we will be able to sit back deserving of rest and joy, we will relax and feel complete. Yet the more we strive, the more we realize that 'more' is the carrot affixed to a band around our heads – we will never feast on all of the 'more'. Of course, it's good to grow.

But, in many ways, we are already living the 'more' we once yearned for. In many ways, we are residing upon the mountaintops we once believed would be 'all' of the 'more' we'd ever need. It's a conscious thing to keep reminding myself of this. I often pause, look around me and say 'wow' to prompt that sense of awe and wonder, be it at the waving branches of a tree in my garden that moves with the wind, that will never again move in that exact way, or the small hand of a child that nestles inside of mine that will one day likely brush my hand aside at the offer. Nothing stays the same, we are growing as we go, and only this moment is certain.

We keep creating our own mountaintops. I think I always will. And as long as I don't buy into the fact that my happiness and sense of deservedness for joy and good things lives at the top of each mountain, then I don't see any harm in tying up my shoes for the climb. However, my pledge is to pause often and marvel at the view from the vantage point I find myself at that day. Whether I spent the day climbing or crawled out of my sleeping bag after succumbing to my need for rest, whether the view is foggy or gleaming with sunshine, there's a view to be drunk in.

Take all the pit stops

A Formula 1 driver could forgo the tyre changes and pit stops in order to beat opponents, yet this wouldn't be a wise decision – it could cost him the race and perhaps even his safety. I feel like I've been that Formula 1 driver in my life, forgoing needed rest in order to squeeze as much productivity as possible out of my wakefulness and energy.

I have experienced burnout and it totally humbled me. Burnout happens when you chronically overlook the limits of your resources. It might be because circumstances mean you are forced to push on relentlessly without the required support. You find your needs overridden and the rest you are able to get nowhere near what your body is yearning for. It may be that the pressures placed upon you come from within, such as a striving for perfection, that furious self-sufficiency, a need to please others or an identity and self-esteem that relies on output to be validated. Maybe it's a bit of both, as mine was. Either way, I overlooked the pit stops. I played the 'when/then' game: 'I'll keep my head down, and then, when this blows over, then I'll rest; when I've got things in good enough order, then I'll ask for some help.' The thing is, one challenge may well 'blow over', but another one is hot on its tail, ready to 'blow in'. I was doing myself a disservice to believe that life would be like an interval workout, with challenging periods and rests. Instead, I have come to accept that life will always be woven with challenges of sorts. It is because of this truth that I open myself up to allow them to let me grow.

I was the Formula 1 car that bypassed the pit stops in the hope that I'd finish the race sooner and be able to slow down, yet I crashed before that relief came. It was a mess. It felt like my skin had been removed from my body, giving every noise and stressor direct access to my exposed nervous system. A simple decision to make about what to have for dinner or the squabbling of my kids was enough to send my body into panic mode, flooding my system with adrenaline and cortisol as if every decision and move I made next were somehow life-or-death ones.

For me, at that point in my life, I had to shrug off everything I'd understood about growing and making decisions. I had to strip life back in every which way, from the work commitments I loved and usually thrived on, to social invitations to spend time with family and friends. The decisions I made had to be calibrated to my low resources to give me time to build up a buffer of resilience to life's choices and stressors.

Becoming sensitive to your needs and limits

As someone who had always sought workout plans and prescriptive steps to growth that I could follow and get 'right', so that I could apply the 'all' of my 'all-or-nothing mentality' and feel a sense of achievement, when I hit burnout, I had to throw this approach out of the window almost overnight.

I believe life had been gently trying to direct me towards the pit stops for years, but onwards I pushed like a determined child who swears they are not tired despite their heavy-lidded eyes and overwrought emotions. Over the years I had worked out through sickness in order to tick 'done' on fitness plans because doing it 'right' was more important than being well. I turned up at the office despite harbouring infectious bugs because I wanted to be seen as a committed employee. Showing up sick felt more important than keeping my bugs to myself. We can overlook, push through and deprioritize the signals our body gives us, until we can't. Until the whispers become a halting scream.

As I rebuilt from burnout, I learned a lesson that will serve me for the rest of my life. I let burnout be my teacher. As well as showing me what happens when you ignore the metaphorical Formula 1 warning signs of smoke pluming from the engine, or the brakes becoming spongy and unresponsive, burnout taught me to look for the nuanced differences between what is self-caring and what is self-sabotaging.

Burnout taught me that catapulting my body out of bed the moment my alarm goes off can either be an act of self-care *or* self-sabotage, and it taught me to know the difference. No plan or life goal is going to incorporate the awareness that some days it's great to push, and some days it's too much. Only we can learn to do that for ourselves, and sometimes it's hard to determine, but with practice, it's possible. When done well, incorporating your humanness into your goals, hopes and intentions could be the best gift you ever give yourself, because it makes them kind and sustainable.

No goal or intention, no plan or prescription, not even my husband lying beside me as my alarm goes off, is better placed than me to know whether hitting snooze would be helpful or hindering, only me. And having spent so many years overlooking and overriding that gut sense of what's nurturing and what's not when it comes to the small and big decisions, it has taken a while to start listening to the whispers so that they need not become a shout. I am better at trusting my gut sense instead of constantly needing to find external validation that I'm doing something 'right'.

This has been another important part of the process in getting to know myself in order to determine which is the helpful or hindering decision. 'You only live once' is the motto we're fed to tempt us to meet wants over needs, to grab the ice cream over the apple (again), or stay for another drink (or three) after you promised you'd get an early night to prepare for the meeting the next day.

Yet, if I'm going to live only once, I want to live well, I want to live fully and I want to make decisions that nurture my future while also respecting where I'm at as I make those same decisions. And to be able to do that, I need to know myself well enough to judge when to roll out of bed and into gym wear and when to roll over into another dream.

Growth isn't just pushing forward; it's knowing when to take the pit stop or the pause. It's knowing when to take a breather to admire the view, to revel in how far you've come and enjoy the highs along the way. Not just when you've reached the top of your current climb, but now, on the step that you're on. Because the present is the only thing that we have for sure.

Day 6

Getting to Know Me

Getting to know myself well enough to determine which decision might be sabotaging one day while empowering and nurturing the next has been so vital in my understanding of sustainable personal growth and goal-setting. What do I even mean by needing to get to know myself? I am myself; how can I need to get to know myself? I remember being in the car with my daughter when she was about three years old. She asked me a question, and I didn't understand what she was saying. I asked her to repeat it, she did, and I still didn't understand. Her volume and frustration escalated as she tried to get across her question, and she began to cry hopelessly. I too felt frustration at our misunderstanding each other, which she was perceiving as anger.

As the satnav competed with her wailing and her frustration intermingled with mine, I pulled into a lay-by, took a breath, turned to her and said, 'Hey, darling, what would you like to know?' 'Is it Tuesday?' she said. My heart broke a tiny bit: all she'd wanted to know was what day it was, all she'd wanted to do was to tap into my knowledge and understanding of the world in the simplest way in order to orientate herself in the week.

Crossed wires, competing noise and a frustration from me that, if I'm honest, moments before had wished that she'd just drop the question. In each relationship there is potential for misunderstanding, misplaced frustration, irritation and hurt. There are overlooked needs and heartfelt words that get lost in translation as we look through lenses that have been smudged and scratched by life's circumstances. For me, learning to know myself has been much like the conversation with my daughter. I have had to change from sitting in the front seat getting frustrated with the emotion coming at me, to pulling the car aside, pausing and really listening.

Instead of stopping and examining my emotions, making space for them and listening to the needs of my body, be they communicated by urgent screams or quiet whispers,

I have got frustrated with myself. I have experienced red-hot rage and dismissed myself as 'angry' when actually the rage is communicating fear and overwhelm. I have felt procrastination and responded with a dismissive 'Why can't you just get stuff done? Stop being lazy', instead of recognizing that the task just feels too huge to start and I need to break it down into more manageable steps. I have chided myself for being irritable as if it were some ugly character flaw, instead of recognizing that I'm hungry, or lonely, and tending to that need instead.

Getting to know myself more has actually required me to realize that I didn't really know myself that well at all. When we're assuming we know what someone is saying without really listening, we can't truly connect with their heart, needs and words, right? In the same way, I had to recognize how I'd been viewing my own emotions and needs through a distorted lens that had been preventing me from connecting to myself.

Unchallenged beliefs and narratives

Through my learning and observing of others over the years, and perhaps from the way caregivers had responded to my needs and emotions, I'd concluded that rage was undesirable and should be quashed immediately. I'd deduced that sadness was ingratitude at the good things in my life, and irritability was a character flaw. I'd surmised that resting was laziness, and pleasing others and being of constant service was vital regardless of the cost to myself. Until I began to question these ingrained narratives and beliefs, it was understandable that I'd respond to my own emotions with disdain and frustration.

Now, with this insight, it saddens me that for so many formative years of my life I didn't really 'see' myself. The child who gets the full force of 'cheer up, be strong, don't cry' when they shed tears at the appearance of a bleeding graze on their little knee, soon learns that strength is praised whereas outward signs of pain are labelled as weakness. So, next time, they cry inside instead. It's as if this process went on within me for years. I'd feel a wave of grief and chastise myself for being weak, telling myself to be grateful for what I had rather than yearning for what I didn't. In time, I believe I didn't truly feel safe within myself.

If my body is my home, the dwelling place for my soul, then how uncomfortable to feel that my own, very normal, human emotions would be criticized and quickly manipulated into something more palatable to the part of myself that deemed them somehow wrong. As I've taken a gentler line of enquiry about my own emotional response to the world, and not shut down feelings that I'd once felt were inappropriate, I've learned so much. I've learned to see overwhelm as a sign of overlooked needs and sought to tend to the need I once would have buried. I've learned to see irritability as a sign of depletion of sleep or nourishment, or an insight into my hormonal rhythm.

Learning the language of needs

At times it has felt like I've needed to learn the language of my own needs, as if I had been dropped into a country with no English speakers or handy interpretation apps. As a therapist I have often sat with those who have chronically overlooked their own needs in pursuit of prioritizing the needs of others. I've sat with those who have compromised their chronic needs as they've opted for quick hits and highs instead to quieten their wants and desires (at least for a moment).

I have learned through pausing and enquiring, rather than jumping in with my usual narratives and beliefs, and forcing them upon myself. It has taken time, a lot of time, and also humility to realize that, as much as I like to believe I know myself better than anyone in the world, in some ways this hasn't been fully true. Observations made by my therapist, my husband and those around me who love me have sometimes shown far clearer an understanding of my needs; they have been able to view and validate the vulnerability that sits just beneath my rage or irritability.

I admit, it hasn't been easy to come to terms with the fact that, in some ways, others have been able to see me more clearly than I've been able to see myself. Most likely because they've viewed me through a lens of compassionate enquiry that has enabled them to see my vulnerability and my need, whereas my lens has tended to be one of self-criticism that hasn't made space or allowance for that childlike part of me that just needs to be heard and seen.

As I've learned to recognize my needs, rather than dictate whether they should or should not exist, I've become better able to see the nuances between the decisions that are one day sabotaging and the next nurturing. Instead of proclaiming to myself 'I don't care if you're tired, ill or needing, you're getting up and cracking on towards the goal I've set you', I am more open to saying 'Okay, let's strip things back today and regroup'.

It's like my inner child isn't so scared of being told off any more. I've begun to feel safer within myself, if that makes sense. I don't walk upon the tightrope of 'correct and acceptable emotion', knowing that I'm going to face my own harsh criticism if I fall off that tightrope. I have no set rules around emotion now – all emotions are there to tell me something, to invite me to enquire. Of course, old habits die hard and I still have tussles with myself as I struggle to remember, for example, that loneliness doesn't mean I'm a social failure, but tells me that I'm craving deeper connection and invites me to consider which relationship I might like to invest in.

Finding forgiveness for your humanness

Sometimes my inner child wins over. Sometimes I score an own goal by letting someone steamroll a boundary. Sometimes I procrastinate my way through a day with full awareness that I'm whiling away precious time and will end the day feeling frustrated at myself. Sometimes I do roll over in the morning and forgo some journalling that I know full well would benefit me that day. Sometimes I do reach for another coffee, knowing I'll feel sick and jittery minutes later. Sometimes my inner child stamps her feet and says, 'Sod the good decisions. Sod the rules and the values, the plans and the nurturing. Sod the intentions and hopes, I'm going to charge right into this unhelpful choice.'

I have found it vital for my own growth to fully accept that sometimes I'll intentionally make a sabotaging decision. Finding forgiveness and enquiry for myself when I lean into a childlike, rebellious 'want' in return for an immediate hit of dopamine, regardless of the cost, has been so important. I have learned that coming down hard on myself pushes me deeper into the all-or-nothing mentality, and finds me tempted to stop seeking growth in that area of my life, because it's too exhausting to walk the tightrope of getting it right all the time.

This isn't about not caring whether I march into an unhelpful, sabotaging decision; it's about not throwing the baby out with the bathwater when I mess up and completely sabotaging the greater heart-inspired goal altogether. Imagine the competitive athlete who scraps her whole career and hopes of competing in the Olympics because one day she skipped a training session for a lie-in. Of course, if this happened more often than not, the Olympic hopes would be nothing but a daydream. But our goal is better decisions more of the time, not all of the time.

The important thing is that when we zoom out to look at the bigger picture, progression is that upward curve, albeit a curve which is turbulent and fractured at points. And I often ask myself this: if my goals can't withstand my humanness, are they truly the goals I should be reaching for?

When I've worked with addicts over the years, the way in which they've responded to relapses has been pivotal in their chance of recovery and freedom. Those who cultivate self-compassion and forgiveness for their own behaviour find it easier to accept forgiveness and compassion from others. Accepting kindness and forgiveness from others is how supportive relationships are built, which are so important for sustainable recovery. Those who find it hard to offer themselves forgiveness for the things they feel shame about find it harder to form those supportive relationships built on openness and honesty.

Self-forgiveness isn't about giving permission to sabotage, it's about using these moments as an opportunity to question whether more support is needed, whether things just feel too much, whether the plan is right for the season and the resources that person has. The more we take this compassionate stance towards our own frailties, the less the relapse feels like proof that seeking freedom is a hopeless cause.

The benefit of tracking and journalling

In the pursuit of getting to know myself better, I have learned to recognize and respect that, in my very nature as a human, I am constantly changing with the years, the seasons and even the hours. A goal or aim that feels effortless one day might feel like wading through thick treacle the next, depending on things both within and outside of my control and awareness: how much of each sleep cycle I've had, whether I've unknowingly eaten something that has aggravated an autoimmune response due to my coeliac disease, whether I'm subconsciously processing a stressful time, or what point I'm at in my hormonal rhythm. It is fruitless criticizing myself for not being as predictable as a simple, well-oiled machine,

because I'm so wildly removed from that as to make it a
downright cruel comparison.

Journalling down streams of consciousness, tracking
my hormonal cycle, seeking therapy and taking risks
of vulnerability and a willingness to have therapeutic
conversations with friends have all been so important
in my journey to making better decisions. As I take
opportunities to turn my attention to my own toxic traits
(many of which are still to be discovered, I'm sure), I
explore my dark corners, my rough edges and even how
tiredness and hormones reduce my impulse control
and cause a relapse in the sharp tongue of my internal
narrative.

Soon we'll be moving towards some journalling prompts,
and I know this can bring up feelings of failure and anxiety
for so many who've tried to journal before and never kept
it up. So use this time to practise your compassionate
enquiry: don't judge, just observe for now – what comes up
for you when you start to think about paying attention to
your own feelings and needs?

Paying attention to the feelings we've been ignoring can
be challenging, but when we see ourselves more clearly,

we can find understanding, we can equip ourselves with tools, we can make allowances where needed in order to be able to thrive. Sometimes recognizing our weaknesses isn't about making ourselves stronger, but allowing others to fill our gaps with their strengths.

Day 7

Jumping Off the Tightrope

I have a strong perfectionist drive within me which can feel so embedded. I believe it's there because in growing up in uncertainty, loss and grief, my coping mechanism was to seek a sense of safety by doing everything I could in order to secure a feeling of predictability and control. Perfectionist me wants to get things right. I want to know I'm on the right track, doing a good job.

When it comes to growth, I want to make good decisions, stay on the path. However, as much as I love the polarization of right and wrong, I've had to learn that growth, just like everything else in our lives, sits in the grey area. Instead of that string-thin, tense rope of 'right' I once tried to walk upon, I now aim to see my growth as a network of paths moving in one direction. Some paths are smaller, veering off and returning; some seem to loop the loop before rejoining. Some are straight and narrow, while others are as wide as fields, meaning that I can swerve and stumble and still stay within the confines of the hedging.

The allure of the black and white, all or nothing

When we've been through times of significant uncertainty or trauma in our lives, the allure of the black and white is that sense of safety and assuredness. There's something reassuringly clear about the tightrope line of 'right', where everything else is 'wrong'; where you know that no matter how wobbly your step, if you can stay on the rope, on the right track, and don't veer, you'll avoid pain or suffering. I've found solace in the 'all or nothing' – I know where I am when I'm all in or all out. When I'm all in, I'm hyper focused on whatever goal I'm fixated on, I'm on track, I'm feeling good, empowered, almost high off the hope. But when I stumble off that rope with one decision I perceive as 'bad', I fall into the 'nothingness', abandoning the cause, the goal, the intention. It doesn't feel good at all, I don't like it, but at least I know where I am, at least it offers certainty.

It's understandable how the certainty offered by the black and white is something we crave, in preference to the murky, confusing, grey areas of life. 'If I follow this plan to the letter, if I live out every bit of advice within the book, if I always make good decisions, I'll be safe, I'll get where I need to be.' Yet we wake up one day and the tick box is no longer promising hope, but calling us a failure instead. The tightrope feels too tight, too thin, too hard to compose our tired body upon, so we slip off.

In my life, having felt like a grown-up as a child, when I grew into a true adult, my inner child began to fight to be heard, seen and appeased. The drive to do the things that felt good in the moment, yet harmed my mind and body, felt too loud and strong. My momentary wants – for dopamine hits and to seek the pleasure of others to validate my existence – took precedence over the deeper ache of my needs. My perfectionism extended to my relationships. I wanted to be a perfect daughter, employee, therapy client, friend and mother. It was exhausting and unsustainable, but at least in a world of uncertainty I knew what I expected of myself.

Growth happens in the grey

Black and white leave no room for tussling, warring and discomfort. They are slick and clear and rigid. When I'm in the 'all' of the 'all or nothing', I'm almost robotic, doing what I'm doing, making the right decisions in order to tick the box and feel productive, like I'm marching towards my goal. I chuck my humanity out of the way, override needs, thoughts, urges and feelings that tell me to slow down, to step off the treadmill of my mission, to stop and smell the flowers instead of seeing them only as a blur in my peripheral vision. And when I'm in the 'nothing' of the 'all or nothing', I'm sitting in the familiarity of guilt, listening to the buzzing soundtrack of self-criticism and waiting for the pressure of shame to build up and catapult me into the promises of a new goal, a new week, a new year.

Challenges are good for us – we know that we don't grow when we're not challenged. We know that making good decisions when it feels tough is when we start shifting old habits. It's in picking an argument with my aggressive, shouting wants in order to move them aside to hear the whispers of my need that I win battles and grow. It's in hearing the words of my ego that I choose to cultivate a more nurturing dialogue. If there wasn't any grappling, struggling, fighting, choosing the harder route over the immediacy of dopamine hits and instant highs, there wouldn't be growth or progress. As much as we love the clarity of the black and white, life is lived in the greys, and growth happens in the greys too.

I once found my familiarity in the whiplash-fast swinging between the black and the white. The rhythm of exciting, fresh promises made to myself, followed by falling off the tightrope into the pit of self-criticism felt like home. Like every other human, I find a sense of safety and home in the familiar, regardless of how conducive to contentedness it is. What feels familiar to you, even as you know you want to escape it?

I have been like the caged bird that, even after the door has been flung open, chooses to stay within the familiar, restrictive confines of the cage rather than fly out to experience the adventure. It's unfamiliar out there it's riskier, but it's also where freedom lies. I have held white-knuckle tight on to destructive eating habits, knowing that they're harming me but fearing that to let go is to step into the grey of the unfamiliar unknown. In time, as I let go, over and over again, I learned to trust that the grey that exists outside of my self-imposed strict rules and goals is where adventure and confidence lie. Not overnight, but over time.

Grappling with control

We are told to let go of what we cannot control, and that makes so much sense. But there is a battle that wages within me, where I see the rope of the tug-of-war of control tempting me, lying at my feet, and my fingers twitch to pick it up. Yet the story of my life shows me that the curve balls that have swiped me sideways thus far were never the ones I'd fretted about and tried to anticipate.

I truly believe that we seek control in the hope we may arm ourselves for the worst-case scenario of any situation. When my sister was dying, I played her death through so many times in my mind, believing that when I faced the inevitable, I might feel buffered from the pain. In truth, when it happened, the pain was fresh and the ground untrodden like virgin snow. Sure, I had lived it in my nightmares and daydreams, yet it didn't soften the heat of the fire of grief I had to walk through. It's as if I planned to embark upon an eight-hour journey. The night before, I slept, anxious about the long drive, enacting it in my sleep. I took every turn. I painstakingly watched the satnav. I marvelled at every change in scenery as I neared my destination. And then I woke. While exhausted from my dream, I still needed to drive it in real time. Sure, my body had lived through the sensations, my heart had raced at the speed and any near-misses, but I still had to drive the drive and my night of anticipation had made it no easier.

Therefore, while I am sure I'll often be tempted to try to find ways to control things that are outside the realm of my control, I'm finding great freedom and empowerment in letting go of the reins. I don't want to break my heart in thought, only to have to find the strength to journey through heartache in real time (if my fear were to come true!). I don't want to drive for hours in my restless dreams only to have to ride the road in reality.

I know that seeking control of the uncontrollable is fruitless, despite how that moment of grabbing the reins makes me feel before I recognize that, of course, the horse I'm riding is galloping to its own agenda. I seek to stop bracing myself for bad things to happen when they aren't. I seek to stop micromanaging that which is more macro than my own abilities will ever stretch to. It's hard, but important, and over time I'm fighting the unfightable a little less.

Over time, not overnight

As I've loosened my grip on control, I've had to loosen my expectation of timescales for growth. In a world where anything that takes longer than next-day delivery has begun to feel like an inconvenience, and a slower-than-immediate reply to an email feels worthy of an apology, no wonder we seek to place timescales on our own growth. No wonder we lean towards the 'How to be happier in one week', 'How to be fitter in a month', 'Three steps to confidence' promises.

Over recent years I have seen an increase in demand for my one-off, solutions-focused coaching-style therapy sessions, where we make quick connections and I draw upon my years of experience to offer a couple of pivotal light-bulb moments to shed some different light upon my client's path. They work, they really do, they kickstart and springboard, but they aren't a replacement for deep therapeutic work – work that isn't just about turning on a light bulb but slowly navigating a whole new map.

I have a long-standing reverence for the immense value of 'in it for the long haul' therapy. The week by week of establishing a relationship that enables my client to turn to face their murky corners, to feel safe and trusting enough to dare to believe the compassionate words I speak because there is no more 'if you really knew the truth you wouldn't say that' left to counteract them. These kinds of conversations have shifted my path and shaped my life. But they take time. And in today's fast-paced culture we are led to believe that we don't have time to spend, so we choose the fast track, the metaphorical next-day delivery of mental health.

I've written many self-help books (of which this, I guess, is one), yet I always hope that if I can take the reader into their first foray of self-compassion and thought-untangling, then maybe they will, in a book's length, begin to believe they're worthy of the deeper chat and work too. In my books I hope to deliver the *amuse-bouche* of therapy that hits the tastebuds and gives a hunger for more, rather than promises to satiate.

We want big stuff to change in our lives and we want it to happen right now. I'm not saying that some of the light-bulb moments, rock bottoms and pivotal experiences don't have the power to set us on a different course immediately, but we cannot risk holding our breath to stumble upon those rare moments. Too much of life happens in the meantime; too much headspace is given to things that don't deserve it; there is too much self-esteem-eroding self-criticism, too many nausea-inducing rides on the shame-fuelled catapult into unsustainable change. I don't want to live like that, as much as our culture tells me I can click to buy transformation and get it shoved through my letter box the next day. I've learned that the marketing doesn't tend to live up to the gritty reality.

All the good stuff in life takes time. Fast-food burgers get flipped moments after hitting the grill, are eaten in seconds, yet leave you hungry and panting for water. The most famous restaurants in the world have you salivating at the table in wait, but it's worth it. Babies take months to grow; summer can't be hurried along; plants strain against the confines of their seed casing until newness is ready to burst forth. Quick fixes feel good for a moment but fall short in the time that follows. We can determinedly chop a rock-hard avocado into a salad, but it's never as good as the one that was left to ripen in the sun.

How can we hold out when the world urges us to storm forward and demand more, quicker? I guess this whole book is about supporting you as you find your ways to grow slow, in the direction you need to grow, at the pace you need to grow in, and helping you be okay with the fact that change might not look like you imagined. Growth happens over time, not overnight, and that's just how it should be.

Part Two

OBSERVATION

Welcome! This second section of the book reads differently to the first. In the first section, I invited you on a week-long meandering journey of my own musing around growth, and in this section the length of the reading is halved. I'll give you some journal points to reflect on and respond to in writing. For the next two weeks, I'll be sharing different aspects of growth along with insights to help empower you to begin making better decisions in your own life in a sustainable way.

As before, give yourself time each day to take a breath and absorb the words, and please don't worry if you take a day off here and there. You have full permission from me to pick up and carry on without guilt, but I'd love for you to give this same permission to yourself too.

Day 8

Values

> 'Values are like fingerprints. Nobody's are the same but you leave them all over everything you do'
> – attributed to *Elvis Presley*

If you gave me your bank statements, online search history and a description of each decision you've made in life, I might be able to establish a good idea of your values (I say 'might' because you can live in conflict with these values). Values are a set of core beliefs and principles that guide our decisions, actions and our understanding of right and wrong. They shape our behaviour, influence our priorities and give insight into what we find meaningful in life. Values can be personal, cultural, ethical or spiritual, and they help us navigate relationships, career choices and life challenges. Values can change and evolve as we learn and experience the world around us and the relationships we have with others.

When considering goals and intentions that help you grow, having a clear understanding of your values means you have something of a map to refer to when you come to the crossroads of decisions.

Define your values

It is said that life is 10 per cent what happens to us and 90 per cent how we react to it. I'm not quite sure where the statistic came from, but I agree that while you cannot control many of the curve balls that cross life's path, you can (or can learn to) choose how you respond to those challenges and experiences.

Consider different values you might have. These are the things you prioritize, the backdrop to your decisions and the heartbeat behind your passions. Some examples are authenticity, compassion, loyalty, fairness, curiosity, generosity, discipline, honesty, justice and tolerance.

Values aren't a list of things you care about like 'my family' or 'getting a promotion', they are the foundations of how you behave. You care about your family so you live out your value of curiosity in the context of your relationships with them. What would that look like in action? Perhaps, instead of shutting someone down for having a conflicting view, you lean into your value, take a curious line and enquire further as to their opinion, enabling you to learn more about their worldview. You might care about 'having a strong body', so you use your value of discipline to implement a routine that works for you.

Cognitive dissonance

Cognitive dissonance is a psychological term for those moments in which you know you've lived and acted outside of your values. Perhaps you've spent an hour scrolling on social media and you get that 'eugh' feeling where you fantasize about throwing your phone out of the window. You feel frustrated that you've scrolled away an opportunity to sleep or to send the overdue email that has been sitting like a weight on your shoulders.

Perhaps that feeling comes after you leave a friend having indulged in gossip that felt fun at the time but has left you feeling empty and regretful for talking about a mutual friend in that way. Perhaps it's the feeling that follows agreeing to another drink when you promised your partner you were just heading out for one. You want it, but you know you don't need it; you feel that internal conflict, but do it anyway.

Begin to note when these feelings arise. Ask yourself what value you were up against in that moment. Refuse to judge yourself, but begin to observe how you think and feel.

Maturity

As you make big and small decisions in line with your values, in the best-case scenario you are doing things for the you of the next hour, the you of tomorrow or next year, rather than giving in to your in-the-moment desires. Overlooking our values can quickly lead to a feeling of unease.

Consider someone who is always opting for immediate pleasure with little regard for backlash. It might be someone who sabotages their Saturday with Friday's hangover, or who speaks out harshly in the heat of the moment, leaving themselves with bruised relationships. You'll also know that person who says they'll do something and then doesn't. Are these figures in your life easy to trust? Do you feel emotionally secure in being vulnerable with them? I'm imagining the answer is no. Yet often this is the dynamic we have within ourselves.

You find yourself doing things you know you'll later regret, leaving a later version of you to pick up the pieces. You make promises to yourself that you don't keep. As time goes on, you don't trust yourself to keep your own pledges or set sustainable goals.

Maturity is when you see an opportunity in front of you for immediate pleasure, yet choose to forgo it in order to walk in step with your values. It may mean delaying gratification or going without an easy ego boost, but each time you walk in step with your values you foster self-respect, self-trust and a sense of safety within yourself.

Decision-making

> 6 **Your beliefs become your thoughts.**
> **Your thoughts become your words.**
> **Your words become your actions.**
> **Your actions become your habits.**
> **Your habits become your values.**
> **Your values become your destiny'**
> – *attributed to Gandhi*

Living more in line with your values as you set your goals and work towards them means becoming conscious of both the small and large crossroads of decisions you encounter and choosing to be more intentional about which route you take. Reflecting on your values will help them to become clearer to you. Then, as you zoom out to look at the bigger picture, it should feel a little easier to make decisions which keep your goals and values absolutely aligned with one another.

If you don't feel an awareness or a stirring conflict of your values when you are being challenged, then perhaps they are not actually your values yet; they exist as ideals instead and they need to be further embedded. To turn an ideal into a value you must live it out until it becomes part of your value system; you must make decisions in line with it and begin to live in the positive consequences of those decisions, so that you begin to really value the value!

As you continue to reflect on your values, start to consider the decisions you make each day, big and small, against their backdrop.

Take a pause

Where in your life do you tend to override your values for short-term pleasure? What might you put in place in your day-to-day life to help increase your chances of making a different decision in future? (Use the shaded areas that follow to note down your thoughts.)

Example: *My value is to have healthy relationships, but I say yes to every social invitation and end up resenting going. In future, rather than accept immediately, I'll say, 'I'll check my diary,' and take a moment to consider whether I've already committed to enough.*

Consider ways you might further live out one of your values.

Example: *I value meaningful connection with others, so I need to be aware when I'm pressuring myself to keep in touch with friends old and new. I am prone to spreading myself too thinly and not being able to fully invest in the few relationships that are the most meaningful to me.*

Day 9

Hopes

> 6 **The natural flights of the human mind are not from pleasure to pleasure, but from hope to hope'**
> – *Samuel Johnson*

When thinking about your goals, consider whether some of them might fare better as hopes and intentions rather than rigidly set targets. This allows flexibility, as a hope doesn't feel as fixed as a goal. Considering hopes instead of goals in some cases is a mindset shift that lessens the likelihood of feelings of failure and disappointment, and creates a wider scope for achievement. Often, the idea of a goal has you walking the tightrope between success and failure, whereas hope finds you meandering and more likely to end up in the vicinity of where you want to be!

Embrace the daydream

What do you yearn for? What are the themes of your daydreams or the wishes you made when you blew the candles out on your birthday cake? Imagine how you would most like to complete this sentence in a year's time: 'You wouldn't believe what's happened to me this past year . . .'

With the advent of smartphones and the ability to fill every waking pause with noise or the consumption of information, the kind of bored daydreaming of my generation's childhood is at risk of becoming extinct. Yet we need these pauses in order to hope and dream both meaningfully and playfully about the future. When you come across a quiet moment today, let your mind wander into the things that bring you joy, things that might shape your hopes and intentions. Popular culture is always offering up ideas of what you should want, who you should want to be and what you should desire to achieve. Yet it is listening to yourself, listening in to the tales spun by your daydreams, that is more likely to give light to which desires, hopes and intentions feel most aligned with who you are.

Reassess old hopes and dreams

Sometimes you outgrow old hopes, they need updating or you recognize that they're unrealistic or you've been wasting precious time and energy to pursue them. Perhaps with increased self-awareness you're realizing that some of the hopes you've been trying to attain were the hopes of a parent, of a teacher, or the desire to follow in the footsteps of someone you no longer admire in the same way.

While grief allows for sadness, it actually paves the way for acceptance. It might be that you hoped to be in a long-term relationship, yet you haven't met the right person. It's okay to grieve the fact that you aren't where you thought you would be at this point in your life. To grieve doesn't mean you collapse into a pit of despair. Truly grieving a loss frees you from the victimhood of 'It's not fair, why me?' It provides the freedom to accept where you are and to instead ask yourself: 'Okay, this is where I am now, what next?'

If you were to go through your wardrobe and put aside the clothes you haven't worn for a while, you'd probably find a few items that no longer fit. Perhaps you'd chosen to keep them as motivation for change, yet instead they just remind you that you didn't get back to that size despite your promises to yourself. Remember that clothes are designed to fit your body; you are not designed to fit your clothes. In the same way, hopes and dreams are best set with the intention of fitting in with you, who you are and how you are, rather than forcing yourself to fit in with ideals that don't fit the curves of your character or the skeleton of your skill set.

Open-handed hope

Consider how some of the good things that have happened in your life aren't even things you'd dreamed for or planned. And take a moment to think about goals you've set that fell by the wayside. The tighter you held these goals, the more the chance for disappointment and feelings of failure if they didn't work out, especially if you didn't fully take into account your humanness as you set them.

Might it be that you plan rigid goals because you lack trust in yourself to grow as you go and to, on the whole, make good decisions? That if you don't grip tightly on to your goal, you can't trust that curve of growth to be upward-turning, albeit bumpy?

What goal have you set that you need to hold in an open palm instead of grasping it with white knuckles, taking any setback or pause as a sign of failure? What would it be like to loosen your grip on your goal and trust yourself a little more in making good decisions towards that goal, more often than not, as they arise each day? Maybe recognizing which elements of your goal are within and outside of your control. What would this look like?

It's great to pursue growth, to hope, to dream and seek. But when you hold these things in rigid fists, you may find that your sense of identity and self-esteem is impacted by the outcome. You may feel success as a high that leaves you hungering for more, or experience failure that damages your sense of identity. As you contemplate your goals today, consider how you might loosen that grip a little and let go of control where you can.

Take a pause

Allow yourself to daydream about your future. Suspend judgement, nudge aside cognition, and see what hopes emerge.

Hold in mind one of the things you hope for. Consider how it's impacting you if you're holding it too tightly. How might you hold that hope in a more open hand?

Example: *I want to be promoted at my Christmas review. Holding it tightly means it's all I'm thinking about and I'll be devastated if I don't get it, but I'm pushing so hard and it's exhausting me. Holding it more loosely could look like asking myself whether I'm pushing too hard, and considering how it might be to 'work hard at the job at hand' in a way that is sustainable rather than working to prove myself in a way that isn't. So, if I get the job, the promotion is based on a pace of work that I can maintain!*

Day 10

Growth

❛ **Acknowledging the good that you already have in your life is the foundation for all abundance'**
– attributed to Eckhart Tolle

While you may meet targets, hit goals and feel the beautiful resonance of living in line with your intentions, it's important to recognize that you will never reach the mountaintop of 'finished'. You live in the messy middle of untied ends regardless of how many you neatly tie, and unfinished to-do lists regardless of how many things get ticked off. You may achieve a clear inbox but it won't be long before a notification pings to alert you to a new email.

When you finish a task, another arises in its place. You can paint the whole house, but a scrape will appear on a fresh wall, reminding you that one day the job will need to be done again. Life is a series of endings that roll into beginnings, that will in turn become endings. Today is all about trusting that you will grow as you go, and inviting you to find joy and a sense of accomplishment as you move along the way, instead of just focusing on what is yet to be done.

When/then

If you have been playing the 'when/then' game, consider what it is that you have been withholding from yourself until your imagined 'then'. Is it rest? A sense of pride in your achievements? An opportunity to lean into something enjoyable? 'When I've reached that level of fitness, finished this piece of work, emptied my inbox, bought that thing, then I'll really start to live, then I'll feel truly happy.' Who knows when your life will come to an end? It certainly won't be when everything has been accomplished. So, how can you get more of what makes you feel alive along the way?

I'll never forget listening to a podcast with a well-known musician who said that even though he'd sold a

record-breaking number of tickets for his tour, he was
devastated to discover that he still wanted to end his life.
It was a stark reminder that if we hinge our hopes of well-
being on meeting an external goal, then we won't take the
small daily steps that our well-being depends on.

Find the glow of pride

Any marathon runner will tell you how buoying it is to
hear the claps and cheers from the sidelines as they run.
They're being praised, not because they've completed
the run, but while they're still running, limping, moving
along the route. When we encourage a child to walk,
we praise their attempts as they stumble and try, we
don't hold off our cheerleading until they are confident
walkers.

In the same way, I encourage you to praise yourself every
time you make a decision that aligns with your values
and hopes, even if it's just a small step in the direction
of your ultimate goal. Only you know the internal battles
you fight in forging a new path, in taking a different
route to the well-trodden rut you're trying to escape.
It's hard to change, it's hard to try, hard to navigate

new ways of being. Your inner child finds comfort in the familiar, so it takes lots of intentionality to change and reach for something different. If you only allow yourself to feel proud at the top of the mountain you're climbing, or with successes rather than attempts, then you will miss out on opportunities to applaud yourself along the way.

Growth in the greys

It's not in reaching the goals that we grow, it's in the reaching *for* them. It's in the striving, the stretching, the carving new paths, that the growth happens. It's in the internal negotiating of a temporary desire to meet a want, over the decision that feels tough in the moment but works towards a greater goal, that you grow. It's in the grappling at the crossroads of decisions that you cultivate confidence, strength and resilience. It's in the navigating of the resulting emotions when you walk headstrong into sabotage that you grow.

While reaching the top of the mountain is an achievement, you'll note that nothing grows on the rocky peak – it's in the valleys where the rich soil produces life. As you journey towards your goals and hopes, you are growing and changing.

As you move into the remainder of your day, regardless of what it holds, recognize the moments in which you feel conflict, tension and dissonance, and say to yourself: 'I might not be where I hope to be yet, but this is growth.'

Take a pause

Consider two areas of your life in which you've been 'when/then'-ing. What have you been holding back as you've waited to reach this goal? How might you welcome some of that into your life along the way?

Example: *'When I move house, then I'll feel happier.' I have been hinging a sense of happiness on moving house. To feel some of that happiness now as I wait for the right house to come on the market, I can think about how I can do small things to my current house that will help me find more joy where I am. I'll start with fixing the leaking tap and painting the bathroom, which I've been putting off because 'one day I'll move'.*

Welcome a sense of pride for something you've done recently. Recognize those imperfect attempts or achievements that feel minor but you know deep down took a lot of intention and effort.

Example: *I pulled out of going for birthday drinks on Saturday. I pushed through the discomfort of saying no and said I needed to have a quiet weekend. It was obvious that my friend felt let down, but it meant I got the rest I needed and I'm proud of myself for that as I would have been at the drinks resentfully.*

Day 11

Coach

> ❛ **If you don't control your self-talk,
> your self-talk controls you. Our
> present talk determines our future'**
> *– attributed to Lou Tice*

The conversation you have within the quiet of your
mind is the single most powerful and influential
conversation you will ever have. Many experience this
inner voice as a monologue, a stream of thoughts and
chatter that ebbs and flows as you observe the world
outside of you and within you. It might say 'I wonder
what's for breakfast. I don't like that woman's hair, why
would she cut it like that? I wish I didn't have to work
today'. It might harshly criticize – 'What's wrong with
you, you failure!' – or encourage – 'Come on, let's do
this, dig deep'. This voice may be reminiscent of a

teacher, a parent. It may carry a tone of impatience or criticism.

Your internal dialogue gives insight into the lens you experience the world through. Perhaps you've learned to give of yourself regardless of the cost, in order to please others, therefore your internal dialogue might tend towards 'I have to say "yes", I don't want to disappoint them'. Maybe you feel a constant lack of safety due to trauma, anxiety or not feeling secure enough as a child. If so, your internal dialogue might sound fearful and safety-seeking: 'I can't try that, something will go wrong.'

Your internal dialogue dictates where you place your boundaries, what behaviour you deem acceptable, how you respond to stress and challenge, how you form relationships. I work with every client to interrogate and reshape their internal dialogue from critical to curious, watching in wonderment as their inner world begins to shift and change as a result, and that's what you're going to begin to do.

Turn your internal dialogue into a person

As you seek to change, grow, address habits and reach for goals, your internal dialogue has an important part to play. Imagine you'd just started a new role at work, where you need to be confident and competent. If I shadowed you all day, critiquing everything you do, you'd rapidly lose confidence: 'Come on, they're watching you! Learn faster, you should know this stuff. You said you could do this job, so prove it.' Imagine the tension in your shoulders from this constant undermining. You'd feel stifled, observed, driven by fear.

Now consider I had a different persona. I shadow you all day and whisper into your right ear: 'This job is new and unknown. If you need any clarity, ask someone. It takes time to get to know a new role, people won't be expecting perfection on day one.' Surely your shoulders wouldn't sit quite so high by your ears? My voice is encouraging and taking into account your humanness. In reality, in the world you'll encounter both, right? You'll come across the encouragers as well as the critics, and you'll have to choose who to give the power to. But if your internal dialogue is already harsh, you'll be more likely to take heed of the critics as this voice will be the most familiar to you, and aligned with what you're already telling yourself.

First voice, second voice

I'm going to encourage you to consider your internal chatter as a dialogue. There can be two voices inside you. The first voice is the immediate response that likely feels most familiar to you. You cannot control this first thought. It's a seemingly instantaneous, reflexive voice that surges forward in response to something. While you can absolutely reshape this voice over time, you cannot control what it says in the moment; you can only choose how you respond to it.

Your first thought might say 'You're late again, it's so disrespectful'. Then you introduce the second voice that says 'Ah no! You're late again. This seems to be a pattern recently, what might we need to tweak or change so you're not rushing out of the house like this? It doesn't feel like a good way to start the day'. The first voice is shaming and critical; the second is grounded, calm and problem-solving.

As you begin to recognize what your first, immediate response is, and intentionally introduce the second, you start to challenge and chip away at the power of the critic. And, in time, as you realize you don't need to be constantly driven by fear, perfectionism and criticism, the second voice will increase in volume and become more integrated. Consider a school: pupils can achieve good grades regardless of whether the teacher controls the class with fear and punishment, or conducts lessons with warmth, patience and openness. Good grades may well be the outcome of both approaches, but the atmosphere and well-being of the pupils will absolutely differ depending on which version of the teacher they have. It's the same with you: you can still grow and achieve without being motivated by self-chastisement! You might not believe me yet, but try it.

As you continue into the week, start to notice that internal dialogue and keep welcoming the warmer, more grounded voice. The intentionality of it all may feel a bit tiring and clunky to begin with, but as it gains volume and confidence, you'll begin to notice that you approach decisions and goals with less tension at the risk of self-criticism and chastisement, and more supportive problem-solving.

Take a pause

Consider the way you speak to yourself. If you could turn this dialogue into a person, what tone would they speak in? What language would they use? What would they look like?

Example: *My inner dialogue would have no regard for my personal space. Although I am female, my inner dialogue is male. He has a loud and impatient tone. Always telling me to do better, to hurry up. To think of everyone else.*

Bring to mind an example of things your internal dialogue says and follow it with a more grounded, encouraging response.

Example: *I locked myself out of my house and my internal dialogue said 'What's wrong with you? You are so stupid. Why are you always doing stuff like this?' A grounded response might have been 'Ooops, this isn't ideal. You've got so much on your mind. A ball was going to get dropped at some point. Let's have a think about our options. Which neighbour has the spare key again?'*

Day 12

Your Story

> ❧ Not everyone will understand your journey, but that's okay. They need to understand their own, not yours'
>
> – *Anon*

When you think ahead about where you'd like to go and grow in life, consider the other narratives that may have fed into your goal or target. Sometimes we can find ourselves continuing along paths that are more aligned with someone else's idea of what success looks like than our own. I have sat with clients who have pursued careers that parents suggested, or stayed in relationships because they'd rather be unfulfilled than ruffle feathers in pursuit of positive, albeit painful, change.

PART TWO: OBSERVATION

Today we're considering some of the external factors
that may have shaped your hopes and aims, so that
you can find more clarity in seeking what is right
for you.

People-pleasing your way off-track

The need to please others will find you deprioritizing
your own hopes and disregarding your own boundaries.
Not everyone will understand the decisions you make or
the hopes you hold, but that is not a reason to let go of
them. If you put every decision you make through the
filter of other people's judgement, you'll never be true to
yourself.

Letting your decisions be dictated by what others
think is a sure-fire way to scupper your own progress
to where you would like to be. People-pleasing in
particular is a multilayered challenge (you can read
about this in more depth in the first chapter of my
book *The Uncomfortable Truth* if it's something you'd
like to tackle). But one tip to help challenge your wish
to please everyone but yourself is to take steps of
authenticity.

You can get in touch with your authentic self by beginning to recognize the ways in which you filter yourself. Consider the things you don't say or do out of concern for what others may think or how they may react. Perhaps you're sitting with friends and you know you don't agree with what is being said, but you choose not to express your opinion because you fear being misunderstood or confronted. This self-filtering is often rooted in fear of rejection at some level. Taking a step of authenticity in such a scenario may well be to say, 'It's interesting you see it like that, I actually feel quite differently!'

People will think all sorts of things about you; you'll be misunderstood left, right and centre. And it's not an indicator that you're doing anything wrong, or making incorrect decisions, it's just part of the human condition.

When you come to the crossroads of a decision, ask yourself which path is right for you, regardless of what others may think. Know that some will question your decision and others will praise it, but only you can truly validate it. Notice your fear of what others may think, and make the choice that is right for you anyway. As you take this step in making decisions that feel authentic to you, you'll develop more confidence in your choices and disempower the weight of other people's subjective opinions.

What would you do if nobody knew?

Next time you find yourself at the crossroads of a decision and you are worried about what other people think, one great litmus test to show whether or not fear of others' opinions is influencing which step you take is to ask yourself 'What would I do if nobody else knew about my choice?' Over the years, I have worked with many of those struggling in the workplace, wishing they could switch roles or jobs. This question is met with 'Well, of course, if nobody knew, I'd leave/apply for a new role'. As soon as my client strips away the worry about letting others down, or being judged for leaving a well-paid job to retrain in another area, they know exactly what they'd do.

I don't want you to get to the end of your life and realize that you'd lived so much of it for others. Not in an altruistic, spending-your-days-off-doing-charity-work sense, but by letting your path veer from what's right for you because of fear of judgement or disappointment. When you allow your decisions to be shaped by the perceived judgement (or very real criticism) of others, the risk is that those relationships become tainted with resentment. When you think about it, that's not fair to those others either.

Wishes over well-being

Making decisions that align with your heartfelt hopes and goals for your life may well disappoint, confuse or open you up to the judgement of others. Something I regularly encourage clients to do is to become aware of when they are prioritizing someone else's wishes over their own well-being. Someone might wish you always said yes to their requests, but doing so in the past has come at the cost of your well-being and you've toed the line of burnout. Someone may wish for you to attend their event or gathering, but to protect your well-being you need a quiet night in.

Wishes aren't concrete needs; they speak of hopes and desires. The strongest relationships in your life can withstand healthy boundaries and a mutual respect of wishes and well-being. Relationships tend to require a bit of sacrifice at times, there's no doubt about that. They can be a graft worth grafting. Yet, sometimes, the wishes of others inflict a heavy cost behind the scenes. It can feel painful to let others down, but it doesn't mean that you shouldn't have held the boundary. When you're saying 'I can't' out of a place of authenticity, you are honouring the relationship, and you are more likely to bring your whole self to the table when you say yes.

As you move on from today's reading, focus your awareness on the decisions you find yourself facing and pay extra attention to the times in which the desire to please others may be influencing those decisions. Remember that you can be kind, caring and sacrificial in healthy ways when it comes to relationships, while making decisions that align with your values.

Take a pause

When have you recently made a decision based on what someone might think, or on how the outcome would be perceived, rather than being aligned with your own growth?

Example: *I am seeking to grow in confidence, yet I keep silencing myself in meetings at work because I know that my ideas are very different to what we've usually done, and I know they will be challenged.*

What decision waits to be made in your life at the moment, be it big or small? Ask yourself what you'd do if nobody knew the choice you were making.

Example: *I have been thinking of moving abroad but have been worried about letting colleagues down and disappointing my parents. If nobody knew or cared, I'd book the ticket and hand in my notice right now.*

Day 13

Self-sabotage

> '❛ I am the obstacle to my greatest dreams'
> – *Craig D. Lounsbrough*

Self-sabotage sounds so counter-intuitive. Why would you want to sabotage your opportunity to accomplish your own goals or successes? Yet we all do it. Consider the moments in which you have self-sabotaged consciously or unconsciously. For example, you knew another biscuit would leave you dealing with a regret-tainted sugar crash. You knew ignoring that email for another day would result in frustrated words from your boss. You also knew you wanted to book that much-needed holiday yet kept putting it off until the flight prices soared out of budget.

Our aim today is to bring clarity as to why you procrastinate and self-sabotage, and start to bring those unconscious acts into your awareness. When you begin to observe those moments of sabotage and recognize how sabotaging hinders you in some way, you're likely to feel more motivation to make more of those positive decisions that help rather than hinder your growth.

The reasons you sabotage

There are many reasons you self-sabotage. It might be that to try something new carries the risk of being shamed and labelled a failure, either by yourself or others, so perhaps it's better not to even try. Maybe you've taken steps to place healthy boundaries and been met with criticism, so as much as you want to try again, the resistance feels too uncomfortable. My book *Know Your Worth* is all about self-esteem and confidence, and would be a good one to read if this is resonating as there is more to unpick.

Perhaps success itself is something that feels uncomfortable to you. You find it awkward to feel recognized for your achievements or want to avoid feeling like an imposter. Maybe the good feelings that come from success feel alien and hard to absorb, so you sabotage yourself as failure and avoidance are familiar territory.

Perhaps anxiety is getting in the way of moving forward. Growth comes through nudging outside of our comfort zones and stepping into territory that in some way feels unknown and uncharted. Anxiety around things going wrong, worry about what others may think and fear of the unknown can all prompt unpleasant feelings that understandably find you wanting to secure safety through avoidance.

The outcome doesn't define you

The world might applaud or criticize you for success and failure but at the end of the day you are not made a better or worse person by either. In his well-known poem 'If', Rudyard Kipling talks about facing times of both triumph and disaster, and not letting either pride or failure distract you from your path. This is an invitation to remember that neither failure nor success move the dial of your innate, unmoving worth.

Both triumph and disaster are reflections of an outcome, a process, not a statement on the core value of who you are. You might triumph in one area of your life and fail in another, and that's the nature of humanness. To hone in on either triumph or disaster is to zone out on the bigger picture of the complexity of your being.

As an individual, you are a patchwork of triumphs, disasters and all that sits in between. Yet if you overinflate the meaning of disaster and what it says about who you are, then of course you're likely to find every which way to sidestep it. Remember that failing doesn't make you a failure, just as triumph doesn't make you an ace at life. As you seek to disempower the criticism and critique of others, it's also fair to disempower the praise and applause that comes from others too. Not in the uncomfortable way that finds you brushing off sincere compliments, but in the way that you acknowledge kind words while knowing that they don't change who you are, they are subjective feedback.

Doing what you don't want to do

Maturity is doing what you need to do, when you don't want to do it. Self-sabotage is doing what we want to do exactly when we want to do it. Sometimes it helps to externalize that part of yourself that wants to meet your immediate desires, cravings and wants. Maybe you imagine what this part looks like, sounds like and acts like. Name it! Some of my clients call it their chimp, or their inner toddler.

When you self-sabotage, it is likely that your fearful, comfort-seeking, craving-satiating chimp, toddler or whatever you wish to label it, is grappling for the reins of your decision-making! As you recognize that this is only a part of you, not your whole being, it offers an opportunity to negotiate and discuss (sometimes even hold a gentle argument), and take the reins back. If you shout and come down hard on a child for holding on to an inappropriate toy, they'll tighten their grip. If you speak warmly and firmly, they'll likely relinquish control. Consider it the same with your inner toddler or chimp. Harsh criticism and shaming work much less effectively than compassion. 'Don't do that, you stupid man' self-talk is more likely to be met with self-sabotaging behaviour than 'I know that's what you want, but you know it's harming the growth you yearn for. You'll be pleased later that you didn't do it.'

What to do when you self-sabotage

When you realize you've self-sabotaged, be wary of turning this into an opportunity to further criticize yourself. Harsh criticism is likely to lead to further sabotage, so instead choose to use this moment as an opportunity to learn. Reflect inwards. It is likely that you are feeling conflicted somewhere within yourself as your outward behaviour and internal goals aren't aligning.

Take time to ask yourself whether the goals you've set are out of reach. Perhaps you haven't properly accounted for your humanness and you've aimed at 'all of the time', when 'more of the time' is a far kinder and more realistic goal? Maybe it wasn't even self-sabotage if you actually ended up meeting a need to rest or slow, or correctly deprioritized something.

Turning towards yourself with enquiry rather than criticism invites you to amend your goals, realize perhaps that you'd benefit from accountability or the opportunity to debrief. Maybe it prompts you to challenge narratives that have been driving you for years, such as 'I never stick to anything'.

You will never completely stop self-sabotaging; it's part of human life to find yourself in a tug-of-war with certain aspects of yourself. Maybe it's the desire to press snooze on the alarm again versus the promise you made yourself last night to get up and ahead of the day. Maybe it's the desire to place healthy boundaries versus the 'It's fine, don't worry' that trips off your tongue when it's really not fine at all. It's natural to negotiate between the pull to comfort and the knowledge that to grow you need to push through discomfort. Keep noticing, keep reflecting, and in time you'll start weakening the blocks of sabotage and realize you're making better decisions for yourself more of the time.

Take a pause

When have you recently self-sabotaged? What motivated that sabotage, what were you afraid of?

Example: *I was meeting a friend I'd not seen for a while and knew she would ask me about recently losing my dad. I was so slow to get ready that I missed my train and had to cancel. Looking back, I think I might have subconsciously sabotaged this meet-up as I've been* *avoiding thinking about my grief and didn't want to talk about it and feel sad.*

Reflect on a recent moment in which you successfully, kindly negotiated with your inner chimp/toddler and how it felt.

Example: *Someone cut me up and usually I'd make them very much aware that they'd crossed me. However, giving vent to my anger has got me into trouble before. I breathed through my frustration and chose to wish them well. It was a battle but I didn't carry the anger through my day, and it showed me I can just let things go if I want to.*

SELF-SABOTAGE

145

Day 14

Energy

> ❝ Trying to do it all and expecting it can be done exactly right is a recipe for disappointment. Perfection is the enemy'
>
> *– Sheryl Sandberg*

As you increase in self-awareness and desire to grow, it's common to feel a sense of overwhelm. You become more aware of your blind spots, your toxic traits, your dark corners, the rough edges of your character and personality, and it all feels like a lot.

As you engage in the world around you, it's common to feel a sense of overwhelm there too. You become aware of all the causes seeking empathy and action, all the campaigns, the changes that need to be made, the flaws and damaging cycles that are interwoven through cultures and generations.

As you gaze at your to-do list, the notifications that ping for your attention, the things that need topping up, screwing in, washing, watering, it can feel overwhelming. There's so much to do and yet you have limited time, energy and resources, so how do you go about life with this awareness, knowing you'll never get it all done, but needing to give it a good go regardless?

You can care without needing to act

You can care about lots of things, but it is impossible for any one person to have the emotional, mental or physical capacity to care deeply about everything. Others may passionately steer you towards the causes they care about, the ways in which they are seeking growth and the matters of their heart. And you may empathize, without needing to give their cause all of your time and attention – it doesn't make you heartless or uncaring. Other issues may carry deep meaning for you instead, and you'll prioritize those.

In the same way, you can desire to tick off all the jobs and meet the needs that come your way, but you cannot do it all and remain mentally healthy. No, scrap that, you simply cannot do it all, full stop. This doesn't mean that you are a callous human, it means that you're a limited one. Sure, you may be misunderstood as you step back from causes or conversations, and that can be difficult. While it's great that a group or a person is deeply passionate about one area of life that needs action and change, we can't all act and change the same thing!

Being led by rage and envy

What angers you? Anger at injustice can give a valuable insight into where your passion lies, offering an opportunity to channel that angry energy into something that does good and fuels change. In the same vein, think about what makes you green with envy. Perhaps you see a friend progress in their job, take a holiday or grow in strength and confidence. Recognizing which achievements of others stir up these feelings of envy can help identify things you might want to grow or go for in your own life!

The priorities that move and motivate you will look different to those that move and motivate others. Put the blinkers on and shun the 'shoulds'. Allow yourself to home in on the ambitions that set your soul on fire and put those higher up your list of priorities. Wonderful things can happen when you allow yourself to be motivated by the things that stir up energy within you.

Channel your energy in the right places

When a friend, social media or those around you powerfully appeal for your heart to be pulled in line with theirs, remember this: you can care about their cause, you can acknowledge its importance, you can be open, touchable, teachable. All of that signals you are an empathetic human who cares about others. Yet at the same time you can also choose to give yourself permission not to dive in headfirst and join them on the front line of the campaign.

If you were a champion of every cause, if you immersed yourself in every campaign which moved your heart, you'd achieve very little. Instead you'd feel overwhelmed and hopeless at all there was to be done. It reminds me of the story of the star thrower by Loren Eiseley in which a little girl is walking along the seashore throwing starfish back into the sea after they have been washed up by a storm. 'Look at all of these starfish, you can't make a difference,' a man challenged. 'Well, I made a difference for that one,' she replied, as they watched a starfish splash back into the ocean.

You only have so much headspace, energy and resources, and it isn't uncaring to choose to channel those into the things that most stir you; in fact, it's wise. You are far more likely to feel motivated to make a difference in an area that most aligns with your values, character, strengths and skill set.

Just as with the starfish-lined beach, you could feel utterly overwhelmed by the number of self-help books available, each of them inviting you to grow and change. Where do you even begin to start tackling habits or advocating for change? I encourage you to consider which habit or area for growth would be a good one to explore first, and channel your focus into that instead of trying to do it all.

Take a pause

Is there something you'd like to give yourself permission to step back from? Or to stop criticizing yourself for not being as passionate about something as someone else? Perhaps it is something on your to-do list that the world tells you is highly important, yet isn't a priority to you.

Example: *I'm on three dating apps because my friends and family are worried about me not finding a partner and are always checking I'm being proactive. It feels like another 'job' I don't have capacity for. I'm really enjoying work right now and it's energizing me. I am going to give myself permission to stop spending time on the apps for a few months.*

What issue do you feel stirred by? Consider one way in which you can stand with, influence, support or invest in this cause. Ensure it aligns with your current level of resources.

Example: *My son has a rare genetic disorder and I feel frustrated at the lack of knowledge around it. It took us years to get a diagnosis. I want to prevent other parents having to endure the wait. I found a small group of parents online who feel the same way. I want to use my skills in education to see if we can invite the specialists we've encountered to help us write a 'cheat sheet' of symptoms and onward referral steps to provide to first-point-of-contact medical staff.*

Day 15

Needs

❝ Needs are few; wants, endless'
– Anonymous

As a child, there was probably a point where you declared, 'I need an ice cream'. In truth, it was simply a desire for the creamy, sugary treat, rather than a physical necessity or true hunger. In the same way, it's common to get our needs and wants confused, especially as wants can feel so urgent and impulsive, like an itch that needs to be scratched, and now. Might it be true for you that often the quick-fix option doesn't really align with your deeper needs or keep you growing in the direction you're seeking to grow?

Today is all about recognizing the deeper need behind the momentary want, and meeting that need more of the time, so you're not just itching itches, scratching scratches and applying plasters for surface-level fixes.

Revealing the deeper need

The want, the desire, the craving, the impulse, tends to speak to a deeper need. Maybe you want to numb grief through changing your physical state or surroundings. Perhaps you want to drown out stress by immersing yourself in information and busyness. Identifying the need behind the immediate desire can be such a gift to yourself. This gives you the opportunity to sidestep the sticking-plaster quick fix. Instead, you can make a decision to meet your need in a way that feels more aligned with your values and growth.

In my case, I might want to increase my intake of nourishing foods. In the moment I crave sweets, yet I know I need something more sustaining and beneficial for my body. If you keep taking the quick-fix hit, you are likely opting to choose the path that hinders and slows growth. As each want arises, you are met with a decision. Do you satisfy the want with one of the myriad quick fixes our culture lays before us? Or do you pause and reflect, and choose to hear the need beyond the want, meeting it now or later in a value-aligned way that allows you to grow?

For me, that would be not only deciding to resist the sugary sweets, but ensuring that I had eaten intentional meals throughout the day, filled with the nourishment my body needs, so that it craves less.

Delayed gratification

Often a want is just a desire to experience the feel-good chemicals of a dopamine hit. The new thing you buy or the end of the biscuit barrel somehow lose their allure and shine once the want has been met. The telling sign that you have fulfilled a want, while overlooking the deeper need, is that feeling of emptiness, guilt or an 'ugh' that often follows.

When a want arises, acknowledge the deeper need and consider a nurturing way you might take a step towards meeting it. Often meeting a need takes more time and energy than a quick fix. A glass of wine takes moments to pour, whereas unrolling a workout mat or allowing yourself to ease into rest takes longer. A flurry of text messages takes moments, yet arranging to go for a walk with a friend won't happen immediately.

Recognize the want, determine the underlying need, and find a way to delay or pause the quick fix. Maybe you set a timer for thirty minutes and promise yourself that flurry of text messages if you still feel the same way when the timer sounds. You may well find that the uncomfortable emotion that prompted you to reach for that quick fix has peaked and subsided, as they often do! As you start to do this regularly, you grow in confidence that emotions are like waves and you can surf them to the shore.

You may find yourself reaching for the quick fix in order to numb or shut down a sensation of discomfort, but in choosing to resist meeting that hunger or yearning with an immediate, short-term resolution, the emotion softens and the wave of urge passes. I use this technique with those who struggle with addiction and in time it can work really well. Not only is the pause an encouragement to feel the feeling and let it run its productive course, but as the thick fog of emotion eases, clarity comes and you're given the opportunity to consider ways to meet that deeper need.

Tapping into gratitude

Next time you feel wanting, pause and enquire. What basic need does this 'want' express? According to Maslow's hierarchy of needs, presented as a pyramid, your basic requirements are for food, water, clothing, sleep and shelter.

So, look a little deeper into your want. What is the basic need it points to? It's often true that you already have more of what you need than you first realized. You might want the thrill of a new car, finding yourself searching on Auto Trader. Yet when you enquire inside as to your actual need, it turns out to be 'a safe way to get to work in order to provide shelter and sustenance for myself and my family'. In which case, you already have a car, you already have a safe way to get to work. This recognition can stir up a sense of gratitude, as so often we take for granted what in other cultures would be an immense privilege. As Aesop says, 'Gratitude turns what we have into enough'.

Now tap into the need a little bit more. Your basic need is already met, so what else is this desire for a new car pointing to? Perhaps you recognize a desire in yourself for novelty. So, instead of buying a new car, maybe you seek newness in another way in your life in order to get that desire for novelty satisfied. Perhaps you clean your car to make it feel fresh and new, or you move some furniture around at home.

Alternatively, you may want a sugar high, yet your true need is nutrition. You have the fruit bowl, you have the stocked cupboard, you're not short of food. So, what is the real desire there? Maybe you want the sweetness or the kick of energy that sugar brings. In which case, what might you do to meet this desire? A quick hit of fresh air? A break from work for a moment to have a chat?

There's nothing wrong in wanting to change your state, shift your environment or seek newness, but sometimes it's good to realize where the deeper need may have already been met in order to prompt gratitude and perspective. And it's good to identify how the need might be met in a way that isn't a superficial quick fix which leaves you still yearning.

Take a pause

Think of a time in which your hopes and goals have been hindered by overlooking the underlying need beyond the immediate craving. How might you respond differently to the need next time?

Example: *I started an evening course as I wanted to change direction in my career. Yet I keep putting off doing the coursework and opting to watch a boxset late into the night instead. I think the deeper need is to address overwhelm as I've not studied in years! But delaying the work is increasing this overwhelmed feeling. I am going to see if anyone on the evening course wants to be my 'study buddy' so we can hold each other accountable.*

What urges are you experiencing at the moment? What might you put in place to delay the quick fix somehow in order to give yourself the chance to meet the deeper need?

Example: *I am trying to stop smoking but keep giving in. I could tell myself I'll wait an hour after having a craving for a cigarette, and I can have one after that if I still want it. I recognize that I have a deeper need to find ways to ease my stress and relieve the monotony of my days.*

Day 16

Accountability

❛ **Accountability breeds responsibility**'
– attributed to Stephen Covey

Accountability is how we take responsibility for the decisions we make, and their consequences. We keep ourselves accountable when, with kindness rather than judgement, we accept and understand a situation as it is, and how our decisions contributed to it. But you don't have to do this alone. Sharing your goals and decisions with others can help you to stay accountable when you're finding things challenging.

I remember moving a huge armchair upstairs by myself. I managed it, but not without straining my shoulder and scraping the paint off the wall. I would have fared much better had I waited for someone to help me. Just because

you *can* do something on your own, doesn't mean it's
the best way to do it. When you're reaching for a goal
and challenging yourself, choosing to go it alone may be
hindering your progress.

Finding others to walk with you offers an opportunity
to seek support and encouragement, to be challenged
and checked in on. Of course, sharing your journey of
growth can feel exposing at times. Letting others in and
alongside you can feel tough to begin with, but being on
the receiving end of supportive words and actions can be
like turning on a light in a dark room. Today is a chance
to reflect on what accountability you have access to and
where those gaps might be.

You are not the sum of your wins and failures

Shame will keep you plodding on alone, whereas
accountability ensures that you have someone to turn to
when the going gets tough. If you find it hard to share the
truth of your struggle within a particular area of your life
because you fear judgement or abandonment, then one of
two things might be true for you.

Firstly, perhaps your sense of self is intertwined with your successes and your failures. This means your confidence is bolstered temporarily by your perceived wins, and dashed by your perceived failures. Perhaps when you fail, instead of recognizing that the decision itself wasn't ideal, you feel like *you* are the failure. It's understandable that you'd expect someone else to judge or criticize you too if that is your go-to response to yourself.

The second reason you might find it hard to seek accountability may be that you've taken the risk of being open with someone in the past and they've let you down or you've felt misunderstood. After that experience, it feels safer to pull up the metaphorical drawbridge and go it alone. For whatever reason, that person lacked the resources, insight or skills to support you. The right person will be able to offer you the support you need, so choose to search again and take that risk.

What does accountability look and sound like for you?

For some, accountability means signing up to an online group or membership to join others that hold shared goals or hopes. It might simply be that you share your goal with a friend, giving them permission to check in on or challenge you from time to time. For others, it may involve seeking therapy or downloading an app.

Who in your life knows about the area in which you are seeking to change or grow? Have you shared your goals with someone trusted and updated that person with how you're getting on? Talking things through is a way to externally process the challenges you face along the way. As you'll be learning, it's actually in the moments of struggle that those new shoots of changing behaviour push through; it's in grappling with the temptation to revert to the old and familiar that you feel a sense of accomplishment in making the harder, but more nurturing, decision.

Who do you turn to in those moments of battling at the crossroads where the old ways shout louder, and the new direction feels uncharted? Debriefing with someone supportive can be great, but having someone to call upon when you're feeling stuck can be just the boost of encouragement you need. When your wants are screaming at you, and the quick fix is tantalizingly easy, having that reminder of your 'why' from someone you trust can be invaluable.

Build the accountability muscle through taking small risks

As you seek accountability, begin to be open with those walking beside you. Accountability is like a muscle that gains strength as you use it. When you seek honest and therapeutic conversations, allowing others to support you and encourage you as you pursue your goals, you are gifting yourself with strength.

You may well be challenging narratives that whisper 'It's best I go this alone' or 'People will let me down'. Sure, you may be able to 'go it alone', but at what cost? Maybe it takes longer to move towards your goal, or perhaps you get there but you feel lonely along the way. Some people may well let you down but that's not an indicator of your deservedness of support, or a sign that everyone will let you down.

Observe the opportunities that occur in which you can be that little more open, or choose to trust someone with a further insight into your goal, challenge or struggle. You don't have to throw open the door to your inner world right away – it might be helpful to know you can just inch it open bit by bit as you grow into a sense of safety.

Begin to welcome opportunities to be open with the right people about your growth and hopes. Verbalizing these goals is a powerful statement to yourself as it reiterates your intentions and is an invitation for much-needed support along the way.

Take a pause

What has held you back from inviting others alongside you as you grow, challenge or change? Remember that the right person or group will be able to support and encourage you.

Example: *I plucked up the courage to tell a friend about my porn addiction as I wanted his support in addressing it. He just played it down with, 'Oh, that's not even a "problem", don't be so hard on yourself.' He normalized something that I really wanted to change, which kind of set me back for a long while. Now I've found a therapist and I'm really changing stuff and feeling so much better.*

Name to yourself a couple of examples of vulnerability or accountability you've taken recently that have felt supportive towards your intention or goal.

Example: *When a friend joked that my phone was lighting up 'like a Christmas tree', I saw the opportunity to open up to her about a late-diagnosed ADHD support group I'd joined. She was the first person outside of the group who I'd told about my diagnosis and how I was trying to come to terms with it. She was so kind and accepting.*

Day 17

Start

> 🔥 Start where you are. Use what you have. Do what you can'
>   – *attributed to Arthur Ashe*

When gearing yourself up for change, it can be acutely tempting to wait for that fresh-start moment. You binge on a Sunday night because Monday is the day you've earmarked for the new diet, or you let your habits spiral towards New Year's Eve because it's your last hurrah before you're 'good'.

There are many moments in life's seasons that come with that opportunity to wipe the metaphorical slate clean, be it January the first, Monday or tomorrow. But these supposed fresh starts can be problematic, because they tend to be polarizing, nudging you into that 'old me, new me, all or nothing'.

The issue is that, as we know, this doesn't take into account humanness, curve balls and wobbly trajectory of growth. The likelihood is that you'll spend the time in the lead-up to your chosen 'new you' date driving yourself further into habits that aren't serving you, before proclaiming newness and then falling at the first hurdle, leading to shame, self-criticism and the hunting for the next 'Day 1'.

As I shared in Day 3, if you want to nurture sustainable change, you need to acquaint yourself with the reset button. So, today is all about giving yourself permission to hit that button whenever you need to.

It's not the end of the world

The danger of a perfectionist, wipe-the-slate-clean mentality is that unhelpful decisions of any kind can have you feeling as if it's the end of the world. If you're prone to this kind of black-and-white thinking, when you find that attitude edging in, imagine zooming out into the bigger picture of your life, until where you are standing becomes as small as the view from a plane window. Then zoom further out until you see Earth as a tiny ball suspended in space, surrounded by glittering stars.

This expansive vision can feel both deeply unsettling and vastly empowering. It provides an injection of perspective. How you feel in this moment is just how you feel in a single moment of time, in the stream of moments, hours, days, seasons and decades. It will pass and life will continue. This isn't an attempt to devalue or diminish your feeling, but to draw your attention to its fleetingness in time.

Reflect on the moments in your life when it felt inconceivable that you might ever get back on track, that you might ever feel content or empowered. You grow as you go, and therefore self-forgiveness is the comforting, strong hand that reaches towards your inner child, cowering in the enormity of the moment, and says 'There is a way forward regardless of whether or not you see it yet'.

Falling into the rut

Do you keep finding yourself falling back into habits that you're trying so hard to address? Imagine a tractor, moving up and down the field, its wheels turning comfortably along the ruts it has slowly created for itself. To choose to change its alignment and forge new furrows isn't an easy job. You could find those big tyres slipping back into the troughs that have been previously created. It would take many repeat journeys over time to create new troughs and for those troughs to feel as comfortable and easy as the old ones.

In the same way, as you address habits, seek change and set goals for yourself, it's natural that your brain and body will seek the path of least resistance. The old path is familiar, even if potentially unhelpful or harmful. When you find yourself on autopilot, making the same old decisions despite your yearning for change, cut yourself some slack and know that the most wonderful thing about your brain is that it is malleable and you can create new neural pathways by repeating new behaviours. But just as defective habits and narratives are embedded over time, not overnight, so it will take time to challenge your norm and find a new way.

It's impossible to give yourself the gift of hitting the reset button and restarting from that present moment in time if you are too busy criticizing yourself for slipping back into that rut. Self-criticism will keep you cowering in that place, whereas allowing yourself to hit reset is like reaching down into that furrow and giving yourself a warm, helping hand right out.

Set yourself up for the best shot

Change requires intentionality, and intentionality requires energy. The more stressed, tired and depleted you are, the harder it is to hold that tractor steering wheel steady enough to steer your way down a new path despite the mud sliding beneath you.

Zoom out to the wider picture of your life and your resources. Are you sleeping well, eating well, doing things that bring you joy? Are you moving your body, having honest conversations and keeping an eye on your general health? It's a fact that when drivers are tired or under the influence of substances, their reaction times slow and their decision-making is hindered. In the same way, when you are depleted and overlooking your own needs, it will impact the decisions you make at those crossroads.

Pick your most pressing need and focus on that one first. It may be tough to let some of the other goals you have slide, but focusing on one at a time when you're making big changes gives you a better chance of success. Perhaps you're always tired as you aren't sleeping well. If so, address sleep hygiene before anything else in order to have the clarity and energy to make other nurturing decisions. The good thing is that as you nurture yourself and ensure your basic needs are being met, so you are better resourced for good decisions at those crossroads we all face. Not all of the time, but more of the time.

As you move forward, pledge to start from where you are rather than waiting for a 'fresh start' moment, and keep hitting reset as needed. Take opportunities to meet your needs where you can so that you can welcome more clarity and intention to those decisions that all contribute to your growth.

Take a pause

In which area of your life do you need to add a reset button? How might adding this reset button change how you approach growth in this area?

Example: *I keep trying to hold boundaries with my phone use before bedtime, but I sometimes find myself scrolling late into the night, then I'm so mad at myself that I think 'Sod it, I might as well carry on'. Next time I become conscious of doing this, I could hit the reset button, put the phone down and salvage what I have left of my sleep!*

How can you resource yourself to feel more able to make better decisions? Maybe it's by challenging a habit or improving sleep quality to give you more energy and strength when faced with decisions.

Example: *I'm currently so busy at work that I'm existing on sugar and sweets. I don't think this is supporting me in making good, clear decisions. I will buy some ready-made* *soup and a pack of rolls on the way to work tomorrow so I have something healthier at hand.*

Day 18

Ambiguity

> ❝ **The grey areas are where you find the complexity. It's where you find the humanity, and it's where you find the truth'**
> *—attributed to Jon Ronson*

If you see your life as a stream of goals, aims and milestones, there's a chance you'll miss out on so much that is happening in the here and now. If you're always looking ahead to the next checkpoint in climbing some kind of 'growth mountain', you'll miss out on the stunning views your effort has gifted you, at the beauty displayed at your feet, right where you stand. Where you find yourself right now, in this moment, is the only true thing that exists.

If you're straining towards the future all the time, you can't relax into the tangibility of now. Today is all about finding more meaning where you stand in life at any moment, so even if your hopes and aims are scuppered tomorrow, obliterated by one of life's unforeseen curve balls, you'll still find purpose.

So much is beyond figuring out

You can seek to control and analyse different facets of your character or progress, yet the truth of it is that even the most accomplished scientists find so much about human form and nature completely beyond comprehension. We live in the grey area of having great knowledge about ourselves and the world around us, yet at the same time with so much being unknown and uncharted. You can pore over information from smart watches that measure heart rate, sleep quality and other data points in order to figure yourself out, but there are an enormous number of systems working at all times within your own body that you don't have insight into.

It's great to want to understand yourself more, to gain fresh insight, to connect the dots, but if a sense of identity or value hinges on you feeling like you have to understand every aspect of yourself, then it's a fruitless effort. You wake up a different person each day, both in the biological and psychological sense. Notice where you are feeling tempted to hold yesterday's accomplishments over today's resources. Notice when you're seeking certainty or predictability beyond that which you'll find, and accept the you that you are today.

Perhaps you feel low, and you can't quite work out why. Maybe you recognize that your impulse control is on the floor, yet you slept well, so it's not tiredness, your usual trigger, that's causing this today. You can either get self-critical and frustrated, questioning whether this is just who you are now, or you can accept that right now, today, for some unknown reason, this is how you feel, and that's okay.

Acceptance allows you to consider what you might do to support the state that you're in today, and work with the resources you have available to you right now. This approach is far more likely to find you amending the decisions you make, the bar of expectation you set and the support you seek. And it's less likely to find you chastising yourself for not bringing yesterday's zest to today, when it's not that you're failing or lazy, it's just that today you have less to bring. Working with who you are today means you're less likely to burn out or face a louder inner critic tomorrow.

How to accept your perpetually unfinished state

A good boss doesn't praise a team only when they bring in business, but takes time to acknowledge and appreciate the hard work and small wins along the way. Similarly, you will realize that even in the trying, the muscles are learning and strengthening, new neural pathways are forming. Even in the failing and the falls, knowledge is being gained. You grow as you go, as you try, fail, grapple, give up, reroute and pivot.

Cultivating self-acceptance wherever you find yourself in life paves the way for more contentedness and joy. Introducing that kinder narrative, and ensuring that the bar of your expectation is aligned with where you are in life right now, are great ways to water the seeds of self-acceptance. Allowing others to support you in the grappling rather than waiting until you're feeling more presentable, celebrating your progression and finding meaning and purpose are also ways to water those seeds.

If you lost your job, your possessions or your internet access tomorrow, would your sense of identity, meaning and purpose be impacted? Likely so. Yet the more you seek to do the things that align with your deeper values, nurture the relationships that feel most pertinent to you and engage in the playful actions that have no other aim but to bring joy, the less you will feel shaken by the inevitable losses of life. You are more than the sum of what you do, what you have, what you look like. The uncomfortable truth is that one day you may well reflect back on your life, and it won't be your job or possessions that matter, it will be the relationships, the mundane moments we so easily take for granted, the adventures you wish you'd had more of.

You will never be finished, but you will never have today again, or this moment. Those you love will never be this age again. Life is finite and all could change in an instant; instead of letting that thought pour fuel on the fire of anxiety, let it prompt you to live more intentionally. As you work on behaviours and habits that move you towards your goals, don't forget to also embrace the experiences and relationships that provide you with a sense of meaning and purpose.

One way that people find meaning and purpose is to give of their own time, skills or resources to help others. Where are you doing this in your life? Knowing that you're having a profound or positive impact on someone's life can be deeply affirming.

Cultivating self-trust

We all have that flaky friend who sets dates and makes promises, yet nearly always cancels at the last minute. You know their intentions are good, but you can't help but be cautious about looking forward to seeing them because their flaky history means you can't depend on them turning up.

Might it be that you are your own flaky friend when it comes to the promises you make to yourself? If you're always failing to live up to your goals, it's easy to stop having faith in your own promises. 'I'm never going to drink again' or 'From tomorrow, I'm holding healthy boundaries' – the more you make promises that you can't keep, the more you erode self-trust.

It can feel inspiring to make these bold promises, ike looking into a different future. But if you aren't surrounding yourself with the right support and seeking accountability, then it makes sense that the promise, no matter how well intentioned and impassioned it was at the time you made it, won't stand.

As you feel yourself straining towards goals and striving for change, bring balance to that future-focused living by choosing to look around you at the joys of today. In many ways you are likely already living out some of the change you once yearned for, and taking a moment to recognize it is so important!

Take a pause

Imagine that you're at the end of your life, reflecting back. What occurs to you? What do you want more of? What did you care too much about? How might you act off the back of this reflection?

Example: *I am imagining that I never got to properly know my dad. I'd want to go back, put our silly differences aside and spend time with him. So, I'm going to try to find ways to do this while I can.*

What promise have you made to yourself over the years that has been hard to keep? How might you pledge a new promise that you can find more faith in?

Example: *I've always promised myself that 'this will be the year' I leave my partner. It needs to happen but life keeps on going and the situation keeps getting more toxic. She isn't open to therapy and separating is going to be awful. I am going to book a session with a therapist to help me approach this and give me accountability.*

Day 19

Crossroads

> ❛ Life presents us with moments of decision – crossroads where we either choose a new direction and move on, or cling to what we already have❜
> *– Mary Buchan*

Today is the introduction of the simple crossroads tool. Each day you are faced with multiple decisions, more than you'll ever recognize. Some of them are utterly meaningless in the grand scheme of life and don't deserve the energy of scrutiny. Do you go for coffee or tea? A simple decision for most, but for a caffeine addict trying to wean themselves off to halt the heart palpitations, it will matter more! This is a reminder of the importance of not looking left or right when it comes to your decisions, but looking inwards.

Over the remaining sixteen days we spend together in *The Good Decision Diary*, I'm going to be encouraging you to recognize those crossroad moments each day. And at the crossroads that hold the most significance for you, ask yourself, when you remember, what smaller decisions lie in front of you. And of these decisions, which decision will help or hinder you?

Tuning in to your gut

As you recognize the crossroads of decision that arise throughout your day, just pause, notice them and consider which decision is more aligned with your values and needs than with your wants and quick-fix desires. Remove any pressure to always get it right or to think that you'll suddenly summon intention for every single decision that you come across. Sometimes the decisions you make are so automatic, habitual and embedded that you may not for a while realize you're making them at all. Sometimes you'll just plough on in autopilot. It's understandable that without intervention or intention you're most likely to do what you've always done.

Remember the inner toddler who shouts for the quick fix? Notice where your want might be shouting more loudly than your deeper yearning for connection, nourishment, nurture or support. The more you tend to the need over the want, the more likely you are to be walking in step with your values and hopes.

Of course, it's hard to know what the right decision is sometimes. Maybe it's not actually a case of right or wrong at all! Decisions are often nuanced and, as much as you might like the clarity of which decision is going to get you the best outcome, it may be that you just have to give it your best shot. One good tip is to hit fast-forward on the scenario. Play the tape forward and visualize yourself having made that decision a minute, hour, day or week later. Does this usher feelings of regret or frustration? Maybe you feel indifferent because it's neither here nor there, or perhaps you recognize feelings of strength and pride.

Choose to tune in with your gut sense and avoid, for a moment at least, the temptation to seek external direction or validation. Ask yourself 'What do I need?' and witness what response arises. Maybe you play each option forward in your mind and see which one feels most resonant with your needs and values.

Shun shame

Self-shaming can so easily be a go-to when you realize you've chosen the path that hinders your health or goal. Instead of unleashing a torrent of harsh criticism on yourself, choose to take an enquiring line. How were you feeling? Was that decision a response to a difficult emotion or stressful moment? Is this behaviour repeated and deserving of some supportive insight or searching for new resources?

Like the 'naughty kid' at school who finds it easier to live up to the label than to try to be seen in a different light, the beliefs you hold about yourself can keep you stuck in a place you don't want to be. 'I'll never change, I'm weak, I'm always going to find this hard' might be narratives that are actually hindering the making of better decisions. Shaming just drives these narratives deeper into your psyche. When you recognize statements like this arise, strip away the certainty. 'Change is tough but possible. I have a weakness but it can be strengthened. I am finding it hard right now, but in time it will get easier.'

Don't grip the map

Believing you need to hit certain milestones and targets, or that your life must look a particular way at a particular time, does one of two things. Firstly, you can end up feeling like life's victim, that it has let you down somehow or that you have failed. In reality, it is highly likely there is a multitude of factors that sits entirely out of your control that have found you where you are. Secondly, the tighter your grip on the map, the more likely you are to resist the fact that perhaps your life could go in a totally different direction that is far more wonderfully right for you than you could ever imagine.

Things you perceive as failures might actually be the doorway to an unexpected adventure. People have shifted whole careers after redundancy, ending up feeling grateful for the forced opportunity for change. People have found partners far more fitting for them, ending up feeling grateful for the heartbreaking end to a relationship. Post-traumatic growth can be the diamond formed in the rubble of dark times. If you think about it, some of the characteristics you most like about yourself may well have been cultivated out of challenge or pain.

So, when you sense your grip on your map, plan or goal is too tense, choose instead to see it as an open hope and welcome those changes of course that might just be exactly what you never knew you needed.

Take a pause

What is a common crossroad moment for you? What happens when you play forward both the helpful and hindering decision?

Example: *I am hooked on online shopping. My finger hovers over the 'buy now' button. If I play it forward, making the decision to buy something I don't need leads to more debt and regret. Making the helpful decision to close the laptop without buying anything makes me feel empowered and hopeful.*

Consider a decision you're faced with. Tune in to what your gut is saying to you.

Example: *My girlfriend wants to book a holiday, and I keep putting it off. My gut sense is that our relationship isn't going in the right direction and I don't think we should be travelling together.*

Day 20

Guilt

> ❝ Take responsibility for your last bad decision, and then let it go. Don't blame others or make excuses for yourself'
>
> *– attributed to Deepak Chopra*

Some days, you will make more good decisions than bad as choices rise up along your path. You will feel proud, accomplished and empowered. Yet at other times, you will walk head-on into making a self-sabotaging decision, knowing full well that you're doing something that is actively hindering or harming you, but doing it anyway. Sometimes everything in you will wonder what the point is in trying to do the right thing.

The much-overlooked key to making better decisions isn't the total eradication of harmful decisions, but how you respond when you make them. Ironically, the more you allow your harmful decisions to teach and guide you in a particular area of your life, the less likely you are in time to keep remaking them. Yet the more you respond with self-criticism and self-shaming, the more you will find yourself warring with that difficult choice. Today the focus is on how to respond when those feelings of guilt and shame arise.

Guilt can direct you

When you feel that rising sense of cognitive dissonance where you're at the crossroads of a decision and you know you've taken the path that doesn't serve you, choose to notice the guilt that arises. Guilt is a helpful emotion that draws your attention to the fact that you've just made a decision that doesn't align with your values, character or goals. It would be a shame to totally dismiss this sense of guilt, as it is there to prompt you to take action somehow. Turning towards the guilt with an enquiring mind ensures that it doesn't just stagnate and turn into shame, where that sense of 'Oh dear, that wasn't ideal' morphs into 'I can't get anything right', making it harder to try again.

So, turn towards the feeling with the question 'What is this guilt prompting me to do or not do?' Perhaps you realize you've said something out of anger that has hurt someone, despite the fact you'd been doing so well in calming your nervous system in stressful moments. Maybe the prompt from this guilty feeling is to apologize to that person. Perhaps you realize your work boundaries have slipped and your rest has been overtaken with projects. Maybe it's time to reassess those boundaries or talk to colleagues about the unsustainable workload. Maybe you shouted at the kids and realize your guilt is signalling that you're depleted and need to get some rest or support.

Working with guilt is like sitting down with a child who's crying, comforting them as you try to work out why they are upset, rather than shouting at the child to stop the noise! It's a way of introducing some compassion and clarity into the situation to help shed some light, so that next time you might feel better equipped to make a different decision.

Choose forgiveness

Forgiveness halts the progression of shame. Introducing self-compassion isn't the same as accepting your own self-sabotaging or harmful decisions and pretending they have no impact. That would be a deliberate oversight of the opportunity to take responsibility, the swerving of a chance to reflect and grow. In short, it's denial. You are sidestepping truth when you reassure yourself that 'It's fine' when it isn't. Ignoring the impact of your poor decisions erodes self-trust and robs you of the opportunity to seek support, guidance or resourcing.

Choosing to forgive yourself is choosing to move forward without being tethered to the past by shame. It's the 'I did wrong there, what do I choose to do next time?' instead of 'I am a failure'.

We are all complex, flawed, and wired to find the easy way out, with more 'easy ways' presented to us than ever before. You may not believe you deserve to let yourself off the hook when things go awry, but choose to forgive yourself anyway, while still holding yourself accountable. Choose to hop back on the route towards your goal regardless of the pit stops and detours you take. Don't sit beside the path – you can't move forward while you're wallowing in the ditch of self-criticism and shame. It might be that you keep slipping back into that ditch because it feels like the most familiar place to be. Just as you forgive others for the mistakes they make, you may have to forgive yourself repeatedly each time you find yourself sliding resolutely back into that place of shame. That's okay, old narratives can take time to shake and can often require the repeated decision to try a new way.

Sometimes choosing to forgive yourself looks like making different decisions despite feeling undeserving of the outcome. It might look like dropping your guard down and letting someone support you, or choosing to enjoy something good in your life when previously you've held back as some sort of self-punishment. Maybe you go after that promotion at work whereas once you'd have let your feelings of imposterism talk yourself out of it.

As a child, if you felt forgiven by those around you when you made mistakes, it may feel easier to forgive yourself. However, if your caregivers held extended grudges, made you earn or beg for forgiveness, or you were made to feel like you were always irritating or frustrating them, you may struggle to forgive yourself. Self-forgiveness is nuanced and worth reflecting on. At the end of the day, if you seek to grow, failing to forgive your mistakes can hold you back because you feel you need to earn your freedom through proof of goodness.

Three-step technique for guilt

To finish today's reading, I'd like to share a three-step tip I created to address guilt. Next time you are struggling to find self-compassion for a hindering decision you've made, use my ACT technique.

1. **A**ddress: Imagine whatever happened as a stone in your hand. Label it, name it. What is it?

Example: *I bought a packet of cigarettes despite the fact I swore I'd never do it again.*

2. **C**ompassion: Introduce some compassion into the picture. What understanding words might you say to a friend in the same situation?

Example: *I have been really stressed at work and arguing with my partner. So I guess it would make sense that smoking would be my go-to.*

3. **T**weak: If guilt is there to prompt you, not shame you, what is it prompting you to do or what tweak might you make with regards to your routine, resources or support?

Example: *I have been meaning to read a book on quitting smoking that has been recommended to me. I think this is my nudge. It's harder than I thought.*

Now you've moved through the three steps, imagine placing that stone down at your feet and walking away. You've allowed the guilt to prompt you, and now it has served its purpose. If it rises up again, keep working through the three steps until it abates.

As you continue on your way, keep choosing forgiveness regardless of whether you feel deserving of it or not. Keep placing that guilt stone on the ground. Keep reaching down and warmly pulling yourself from that ditch that runs alongside the long and winding track of growth.

Take a pause

When has it felt inconceivable that you might move on from a harmful or less-than-ideal decision? Note down areas of growth that followed.

Example: *I cheated on my husband. It was the worst decision of my life and I didn't think our relationship would ever feel normal again. We went straight to therapy and through that process addressed dynamics that we'd struggled with for years. We are happier than we could ever have been. It was excruciating for a while, but we learned stuff about ourselves that is going to benefit us forever.*

Work through the three steps with something you have felt guilty about recently.

Day 21

Perseverance

> 6 **Fall down seven times and stand up eight'**
> – *Japanese proverb*

As this section of your book draws to a close, I want to gift you with some encouraging words to help you keep on keeping on. From tomorrow you will simply spend your journalling time reflecting on the decisions you've made each day, introducing some self-compassion and self-coaching where needed, with less of my guidance. Making journalling your own will, I hope, turn it into a habit for life.

My wish is that this journey will set you up to approach your own growth in a fresh and sustainable way that will benefit you for years to come. I hope that through these daily readings you have been able to fine-tune your goals, hopes and intentions to take into account your humanness and the inherently imperfect nature of growth itself. As you continue to adapt and amend your goals and ambitions in the future, you'll pave the way for more contentedness and more openness for life to develop in ways you wouldn't imagine.

Look back to move forward

I don't know about you, but when I look back at my life, many of the things I love about my character were born out of brokenness. Time is your greatest ally in granting perspective on how you grow and change for the better. Day by day, it can seem like little is changing, yet as you make more decisions in line with your values, over time you'll look back to see that so much has shifted along the way. Take a moment to reflect on how life has shaped, challenged and grown you in ways you wouldn't have planned or imagined it would or could. Use this as inspiration for future change.

Each nurturing decision has value, no matter how small

If you were to go to the gym and lift weights daily, you'd grow in strength pretty fast. Yet if you went twice a week, you'd still grow in strength. Less strength perhaps, and at less speed, but growth all the same. Some years ago, with my all-or-nothing mentality in full force, I'd think 'What's the point in exercising once a week?' There *is* a point. One nurturing act is far better than no nurturing acts; one exercise of strength is more beneficial than none. One open and honest conversation is going to deepen a connection more than if you'd kept silent. One step forward is still one step closer than you were before.

If your narrative around making positive changes has been focused on how fast and how hard you can get there, as it tends to be in our wider culture, it's understandable that you might feel tempted to devalue or diminish the small act, the small step, the small change. I encourage you not to overlook those small, positive decisions, even if they sit in the wider context of numerous sabotaging, hindering ones. That one small good decision could be the green shoot that makes its way through the muddy ground and prompts new hope, you never know.

If you can't keep on, you're pushing too hard

Where you feel resistance towards the change you want to make, listen in. Changing habits disrupts our status quo and therefore tends to require energy, headspace, support and intention. Yet if you feel like you're having to push too hard, and you're too often finding yourself down in that ditch beside the path of growth, it might be that the path you keep trying to climb upon isn't the right one for you to walk right now. Or perhaps you need someone to walk alongside you on it for support.

Review your hopes and goals. Question whether you have the resources you need to make the necessary changes, or whether the goal is perhaps too ambitious, finding you straining towards it and repeatedly collapsing in exhaustion. Yes, change requires a lot of strength sometimes, but if it's too hard, maybe it's because too much is being asked of you this time, as if you're picking up a load you are not strong enough (yet) to carry. Maybe the goal is right for you at this time, but you've been trying to go it alone, and you need support or accountability.

If your goal is to address an addiction or a habit that you find yourself compulsively repeating regardless of the later cost, it will be beneficial to seek additional support. What pain might be fuelling some of your harmful decisions? What habits do you keep turning towards when difficult feelings arise, or you face stress or anxiety?

Addiction is a way to respond to feelings you'd rather not feel, such as hurt, grief, stress or overwhelm. Despite the longer term or immediate physical or mental consequences, addiction will find you driven to do something over and over for that quick-fix, short-term relief. If this resonates for you, the right support will mean that change stops feeling like such a relentless uphill battle that keeps leaving you in a heap at the bottom. Turn to the Helpful Contacts section on p. 287 for places to find the help you need.

The importance of rest

Just as nature appears to pull back and lie dormant in order to burst forth in spring with new zest, expect to find yourself in slower seasons, months or days. If you are going through a challenging, stressful or painful time, your mind and body will be focusing on digging deep and making it through. You may well have less energy to invest in forming new habits and reshaping old ones.

Continuing to journal, reflect and have intentional conversations will ensure that if you are in a season of turning inwards, of hibernation and slowness, you remain open and accountable along the way. Just as it may well look like trees are giving up on life as they shed their leaves, or that hibernating animals are totally dormant, in truth, they are resting to re-energize and move forward with strength. Turning inwards and seeking solitude when needed, for as long as needed, may look unproductive, but in truth carries such an important purpose. Remember this, and know that intentional accountability and reflection as you do so will ensure your slowing-down is restorative, and reduces the risk of sliding into stagnation or isolation.

Moving on

As you step into the next section of *The Good Decision Diary*, hold in mind the fact that growth is a dance, not a straightforward onward walk of consistency. You're dancing a complex, haphazard sequence of stumbles, slow sways, heart-racing quickstep, pauses and solo moves. The beautifully choreographed flows into the chaotically improvised. One moment you're dancing fluidly with a partner before finding yourself joined by a troupe and an audience, and then being left to dance in the silence and dark alone.

As you move into daily reflection on your goals and the decisions you make, just remember that there is no road map for change. As much as you might crave the certainty of knowing the right way to go, you're not doing it 'wrong' any more than you might like to be commended for doing it 'right'. You're just growing as you go.

Take a pause

Reflect on the years gone by. How have you grown along the way in expected or unexpected ways?

Example: *I used to be terrified of public speaking. I'd forgotten totally about that! My team got restructured a couple of years ago, and either I had to start presenting client pitches or find a new job. Public speaking feels second nature to me now, a far cry from where I was.*

Consider the last time you felt a need to slow down, to metaphorically hibernate or turn inwards. What purpose did this have for you? Next time, how might you ensure that you remain attentive to yourself throughout this slowness and reduce the risk of stagnation or isolation?

Example: *Last winter I slowed down when everyone else was speeding up. We had a stripped-back Christmas, which was so good. When I feel overwhelmed, and like I need to retreat a bit, I have to make sure I keep talking to my closest friend about how I feel.*

Part Three

CHANGE

———

In this third and final section of *The Good Decision Diary*, the focus is on nurturing sustainable change through the daily decisions you face. I invite you to spend five to ten minutes at the end of each day answering a short set of questions to reflect on your day. As you journal about your decisions over the next two weeks, you will begin to see patterns emerging and chances to make different – better – choices for yourself, more of the time.

Each day is laid out in the same way, offering you the opportunity to reflect on how the day went, as well as to get curious about where you might make different decisions next time. Each day I will offer you a short sentence or mantra to hold in your mind, and a little bit of guidance around this mantra. In time, you will be able to come up with your own daily mantra.

I will also ask you to check in with your energy levels each day, as your energy levels will impact the resources you have available and how well equipped you are to make changes.

For example: *I didn't sleep well last night and think I might be coming down with something. All day long I have craved comfort, caffeine and quick fixes.*

Then you will reflect on two decisions you've made over the course of the day – if you want to reflect on more decisions, then be my guest! I'd suggest focusing on one decision you feel you made in alignment with your goals, and one where you wish, in retrospect, you had chosen differently. Ask yourself whether you need support with your goals and decisions, or perhaps more resources.

Here are two examples:

Decision I'm Proud Of

The decision I made: *I was about to shout at my kids for leaving their muddy shoes in the hallway and making a mess. Instead, I took a deep breath*

and calmly asked them to put their shoes away,
which they did with less fuss than I had expected.

Reflection on my decision: *It's always an issue
for me when they come in with dirty shoes on.
Sometimes just the sound of the door opening
is enough for me to anticipate the mess and get
irritated before I've even said hello.*

How to move forward: *I'm going to get some shelves
for outdoor shoes and put them by the front door, so
that the kids have a place to put their shoes out of
the way. I will ask for help with this from my partner.*

Decision I'd Like to Have Made Differently

The decision I made: *My colleague criticized my
work in a way that I found hurtful and unhelpful.
I didn't say anything back to their criticism. I just
felt annoyed.*

Reflection on my decision: *I am frustrated that I didn't speak up as I've been trying to work on being more authentic and honest rather than just swallowing my words. I'm feeling unwell, though, so didn't feel up to having a difficult conversation today.*

How to move forward: *I could send my colleague an email on Monday, or ask for a quick chat to share my points in a considered way once I feel less angry.*

Did Guilt Feature in My Day?

(Here is a chance each day to address any residual guilt using the three-step ACT technique.)

Address: *Label your guilt.*

Compassion: *What compassionate words can you add?*

Tweak: *If guilt is there to prompt you, what is it prompting you to do?*

Example:

Address: *I feel guilty for snapping at my partner this evening.*

Compassion: *I haven't been feeling 100 per cent and was carrying anger after receiving badly worded, negative criticism at work.*

Tweak: *I am going to apologize to my partner and let her know the situation at work so that she understands the context.*

Tomorrow's intention: (Here, write down a note of intention for tomorrow. It may be that you want to address a certain habit or seek to continue positive change. Remember to hold this in open hands rather than a tight grip – it's a kind intention, not a stick to beat yourself with.)

Example: *I am going to accept opportunities to slow down, rest and recover.*

Day 22

MANTRA *The decisions I make reflect the values I hold*

Let your mind settle on one of the decisions you were faced with today. Was the choice you made reflective of the values you hold? Or did it prompt that uneasy sense of conflict that comes with not living in line with who and how you want to be?

Which choices have you made today that left the later version of you to pick up the pieces in some way? And which decisions you made were the ones that placed a solid building block in the bigger picture of your vision and hopes for yourself and your life? While it's tempting to zone in on the decisions that lean towards self-sabotage, don't forget that with each good and nurturing decision, you are taking a step forward, in line with your values, and placing a piece of the puzzle to help the bigger picture emerge.

If you often find yourself making choices that don't reflect the values you hold dear, or you consistently find yourself reaching for the momentary hit, consider where the gaps might be in your support network or really spend time journalling around why that value is so important to you, to help reinforce it.

Today's energy levels:

Decision I'm Proud Of

The decision I made:

Reflection on my decision:

How to move forward:

Decision I'd Like to Have Made Differently

The decision I made:

Reflection on my decision:

How to move forward:

Did Guilt Feature in My Day?

Address:

Compassion:

Tweak:

Tomorrow's intention:

Day 23

MANTRA *When I set goals, I remember to make space for my humanness*

As you've moved through your day, have you noticed any of your goals that could do with a little extra flexibility to account for your humanness? How have you taken into account your energy levels, your resources and your level of motivation today as you've made choices? Or perhaps you've recognized that something you've been striving for just doesn't fit with this season's version of you, like an old pair of jeans you keep putting on no matter how uncomfortable they make you feel.

Taking a flexible, gentle approach to growth and decision-making can feel alien in our goal-orientated, output-focused culture. Perhaps, if you're honest, you believe that if you choose to work with who you are today, it might somehow weaken who you are tomorrow. Yet if you soften your expectations today to account for exhaustion or overwhelm, then it may well be that you wake up tomorrow more energized and able to push ahead productively. You grow in trust as you choose to walk in step with who you are today.

Have you enjoyed daydreaming today? If not, spend a moment right now letting your mind wander back over your life in awe at some of the unexpected, wonderful things that have sprung from choices you've made. And then let it meander into your future, to hope and dream of all that may come.

Today's energy levels:

Decision I'm Proud Of

The decision I made:

Reflection on my decision:

How to move forward:

Decision I'd Like to Have Made Differently

The decision I made:

Reflection on my decision:

How to move forward:

Did Guilt Feature in My Day?

Address:

Compassion:

Tweak:

Tomorrow's intention:

Day 24

MANTRA *I am growing as I go. I don't need to micromanage every decision*

Today you have lived in life's messy middle, you have navigated the grey areas, and you've made your way through the cascade of endless errands and calls upon your resources. You may well have rounded some things off neatly, but you'll also have some unfinished business and untied ends. That isn't a sign of your failure to be productive, but instead is a symptom of being a human in a world that never stops moving.

How have you found joy along the way today? Have you slowed down enough to embrace a moment of awe at nature, or allowed yourself to feel a swell of pride in how far you've come as you've reached to make more good decisions? If so, how has this benefited you?

As you reflect, recognize where you've held off meeting a need or taking a craved-for break until you've reached a goal or target or completed your (ultimately uncompletable) to-do list. What needs have gone unmet, and what feelings or stresses might you acknowledge and create space for? Notice the temptation to diminish or analyse any of those feelings, and choose to listen openly to yourself without judgement as you would someone you care about.

Today's energy levels:

Decision I'm Proud Of

The decision I made:

Reflection on my decision:

How to move forward:

Decision I'd Like to Have Made Differently

The decision I made:

Reflection on my decision:

How to move forward:

Did Guilt Feature in My Day?

Address:

Compassion:

Tweak:

Tomorrow's intention:

Day 25

MANTRA I choose motivating self-encouragement over shaming self-criticism

How has your internal dialogue sounded as you've moved through your day? Has it erred on the side of critical, shaming and bullying, or nurturing, warm and coaching? Or maybe it has teetered somewhere between the two, shifting between the kind and the critical. As you spend a moment thinking, recognize whether you're appraising your day with 'I should have tried harder', and offer up the softened approach of 'Challenging my internal narrative is tough! I'm so glad I'm working on this'.

Keep introducing that second, alternative, warmer narrative. Notice where frustration arises when it feels effortful or is taking time, for that is the nature of the beast! It takes time to turn a ship around, and sometimes it can feel like you're having to heave it, but rest assured, you're slowly changing the course of this powerful inner conversation, and you'll glean the benefits over time, not overnight. As you begin to notice how you talk within the quiet of your mind, and introduce that more grounded voice, you'll notice that before too long that voice of warm guidance will come forth more often when you find yourself at those big and small decision points in your day.

Today's energy levels:

Decision I'm Proud Of

The decision I made:

Reflection on my decision:

How to move forward:

Decision I'd Like to Have Made Differently

The decision I made:

Reflection on my decision:

How to move forward:

Did Guilt Feature in My Day?

Address:

Compassion:

Tweak:

Tomorrow's intention:

Day 26

MANTRA *I choose to consider my well-being in the decisions I make today*

As you're moving into the final part of your day, if you have deprioritized your well-being in some way today, in pursuit of fulfilling someone else's wishes or out of a need to please someone, how might you tend to your well-being right now in a small way? Perhaps you overlooked a need to rest, so you opt for some screen-free time and head to bed early. Maybe you've silenced your voice somehow, so you ask a friend to meet for a chat over the coming days in order to have your voice heard and validated.

Consider the decisions you've made, not just today but in your life to date. Where have you honoured the whisper of your well-being by placing a boundary or making the better decision for yourself even though you wished for the easy-out or the quick fix? Where have you sidestepped the fear of worrying about what others might think and made a decision that feels authentic to you? It's not always the easy choice, but as you do this, you strengthen and empower yourself to make more of those decisions. You will see how healthy relationships can withstand healthy boundaries, and you will begin to benefit from the outcomes of good, but sometimes tough, choices.

Today's energy levels:

Decision I'm Proud Of

The decision I made:

Reflection on my decision:

How to move forward:

Decision I'd Like to Have Made Differently

The decision I made:

Reflection on my decision:

How to move forward:

Did Guilt Feature in My Day?

Address:

Compassion:

Tweak:

Tomorrow's intention:

Day 27

MANTRA *I deserve to thrive*

Where today have you made the decision not to self-sabotage where you might usually do so? How did it feel afterwards? What are the fruits of that decision? Acknowledge that the nurturing choice may well have been a difficult decision that required you to dig deep for strength and keep your vision fixed on the bigger picture of where you yearn to be.

Each time you choose not to self-sabotage in an area where you have historically taken the path of least resistance (albeit at a higher cost over time), imagine the habit as a thick glass monument sitting in your front garden, obscuring your view and hindering the sunlight from streaming through your window. Each time you make a nurturing decision, you are tapping on the glass structure of that habit or behaviour with a small metal hammer. You might feel disenchanted as you want the glass to shatter and fall all at once. But rest assured, each small tap is disturbing the bonds that hold the structure together. Sometimes you might see huge chunks of glass fall away, but even when it looks like nothing is happening, you are sending hairline fissures throughout, weakening it bit by bit, until it collapses and the view is clear.

If you're looking back over your day and your focus is fixed only on the times you walked straight into self-sabotage, consider whether your goal was set too high. Maybe your support network requires some gap-filling, or you're just tired and depleted and resolve was low. Either way, the self-sabotaging decision gives insight into a need you can choose to meet now, in a way that serves and nurtures you. Offer acknowledgement in place of the momentary self-abandonment. While you might not have tapped on that glass structure with your little hammer in that specific choice you made, all is certainly not lost.

Today's energy levels:

Decision I'm Proud Of

The decision I made:

Reflection on my decision:

How to move forward:

Decision I'd Like to Have Made Differently

The decision I made:

Reflection on my decision:

How to move forward:

Did Guilt Feature in My Day?

Address:

Compassion:

Tweak:

Tomorrow's intention:

Day 28

MANTRA *Perfectionism is the thief of growth*

Casting your mind back over your day, where has perfectionism nudged up your bar of self-expectation and left you falling short? Where might you have applied perfectionism to this process of choosing to make more positive decisions? Commend yourself for the growing desire to approach moments of decision with more intention and consciousness, but remind yourself of the truth that you can't grow in every which way all the time. And accept that you will never be fully 'grown'.

Which area of your life deserves the most focus at the moment? Which habit needs the most urgent attention in order for you to find fresh freedom? Directing your focus on one or two specific areas doesn't mean that you're 'giving up' on the other areas of life that need some attention, it just means you're not spreading your energy too thinly. Working on one or two habits or challenges at a time means that as you sense things shift, you feel accomplished and motivated! Maybe you choose to increase your water intake as you've been getting headaches. Focus on that first and once you're at a place where you are feeling more cucumber than prune, and it's second nature to pick up your water bottle along with your house keys, then the sense of accomplishment will fuel you to tackle the next thing. There is no race, there is no finish line. It's just you, trying to make one extra nurturing decision around that one thing than you did yesterday.

Today's energy levels:

Decision I'm Proud Of

The decision I made:

Reflection on my decision:

How to move forward:

Decision I'd Like to Have Made Differently

The decision I made:

Reflection on my decision:

How to move forward:

Did Guilt Feature in My Day?

Address:

Compassion:

Tweak:

Tomorrow's intention:

Day 29

MANTRA *I will consider the deeper need beneath my impulse*

Many of the decisions you faced today had you standing at the crossroads of the quick-fix hit versus the choice that likely felt like the harder road to take, but would benefit you in the longer term. As you reflect back on your day, it is all too easy to lean into self-criticism for the decisions you made that didn't support you in getting where you want to go.

Resist the temptation to label them 'bad' and choose instead to take the warm, enquiring approach as to what needs or feelings sat beyond those cravings for the quick fix. Even if you opted for the quick fix, as you look into the days ahead, how might you go some large or small way to meet that deeper need? Or might you benefit from implementing a pause mechanism (such as setting a timer) to add in a moment of delay to that quick surface-level gratification?

As for those decisions you made today that might have felt like a victorious tug-of-war between want and need, conjure a sense of self-congratulations or a glow of pride. Your inner child will delight at that recognition, despite how false it may feel if your usual dialogue takes a negative bias. In time, congratulating yourself will become easier as that internal dialogue becomes more supportive.

Today's energy levels:

Decision I'm Proud Of

The decision I made:

Reflection on my decision:

How to move forward:

Decision I'd Like to Have Made Differently

The decision I made:

Reflection on my decision:

How to move forward:

Did Guilt Feature in My Day?

Address:

Compassion:

Tweak:

Tomorrow's intention:

Day 30

MANTRA *Accountability is vital for growth.*
Vulnerability is vital for accountability

Was there a moment today when you might have benefited
from sharing your thoughts or feelings with someone else?
Was there a decision that you may have made differently if
you'd asked someone to give you some supportive words?
If you overlooked that need or sidestepped an opportunity
to talk more openly, debriefing with a trusted person can
be a great way to externally process that scenario and
welcome valuable perspective and insight.

Is there an area in which you feel you'd benefit from the
voices of others who are on a similar path to you? Consider
what might be holding you back from seeking that support,
and also how it might feel to be validated and encouraged
by others who get how it feels to face your specific
challenge and may be further down that path than you.
Consider how you might take a step towards finding that
community or deepening an existing relationship through

taking those small risks of vulnerability and openness. Never underestimate the power of sharing your story with others either. Openness breaks shame and taboo, and offers an opportunity to drop masks and experience richer, therapeutic connection with others. You deserve it all!

Today's energy levels:

Decision I'm Proud Of

The decision I made:

Reflection on my decision:

How to move forward:

Decision I'd Like to Have Made Differently

The decision I made:

Reflection on my decision:

How to move forward:

Did Guilt Feature in My Day?

Address:

Compassion:

Tweak:

Tomorrow's intention:

Day 31

MANTRA   *I can create new habits and neural pathways*

Was there a moment today in which you found yourself opting for the path of least resistance, even though you've been trying so hard to make better decisions in that area of your life? This is going to happen and will form the bumps in that upward, jagged line of growth. Just as the huge tractor tyres slip back into familiar furrows when trying to forge a new path, remember that it will take time to establish new habits and form those new neural pathways that will find you making better decisions more of the time . . . in time.

Don't forget to gift yourself a shiny red reset button that you can hit each time you slide back into the familiar furrows. When you're tempted to shame and criticize yourself for your perceived failure, hit the reset button and don't let that one decision leave you feeling defeatist against the next.

As you reflect on your day, was there anything you did that really helped set you up to make good decisions? Perhaps you chose the lie-in over the productive early start because you knew rest was a priority. Maybe you called a friend to chat through your stress to help you in your battle against the post-work booze. Recognize the actions or people that helped support you in making good decisions and consider what might help you meet some of those good-decision-supporting needs tomorrow too.

Today's energy levels:

Decision I'm Proud Of

The decision I made:

Reflection on my decision:

How to move forward:

Decision I'd Like to Have Made Differently

The decision I made:

Reflection on my decision:

How to move forward:

Did Guilt Feature in My Day?

Address:

Compassion:

Tweak:

Tomorrow's intention:

Day 32

MANTRA I wake up as a different version of myself every day

You woke up a different version of yourself to the you that woke up yesterday. You are an ever-changing entity impacted, shaped and resourced by things both within and outside of your control. It's beneficial to hold an awareness of the narrative in your mind and the feelings that sit around the decisions you are faced with, but alongside that, cultivate an attitude of acceptance that you'll never feel finished.

Your ends will never feel fully tied. That can seem like a defeatist attitude to hold when culture applauds striving and pushing forward, but when you think over times in your life when you've pushed and pushed, can you recognize you were perhaps lacking in that joy and rest you so need in order for growth to be sustainable?

Along with striving to make good decisions, choose also to do things that feed your sense of identity, purpose,

connection and joy. Choose to invest in the things that
sit outside of the realm of worldly growth in financial or
material goals, the things that bring a deeper sense of
purpose. So, in light of that invitation, what decision have
you made today that you feel proud of? Perhaps you
chose to do something that felt challenging yet aligns
with your values. Maybe you made a decision that enabled
you to connect with someone important to you, or chose
to inject some much-needed joy or rest into your day.
Joy and rest may well feel unproductive, but they are
energizing and therefore will later support you in those
moments of decision that punctuate your day.

Today's energy levels:

Decision I'm Proud Of

The decision I made:

Reflection on my decision:

How to move forward:

Decision I'd Like to Have Made Differently

The decision I made:

Reflection on my decision:

How to move forward:

Did Guilt Feature in My Day?

Address:

Compassion:

Tweak:

Tomorrow's intention:

Day 33

MANTRA *I choose to hold my goals in open hands*

Where today have you tuned in to your gut sense when you faced a decision? Or where do you think you completely overlooked that quiet whisper as you turned to the internet or a friend before giving it a second thought? If you overlooked it, tune in to it now and consider what decision you might have made had you listened in to your needs and sense of what was the best choice for you. Perhaps you'd like to spend a moment reflecting on times in which that gut sense has led the way to a place you wouldn't have otherwise been.

Whether you're someone who maps out a step-by-step route to get you to where you want to be or promises to make 'better decisions from this point onwards', how can you loosen your grip on control as you move forward into tomorrow? Choose to turn inwards to that quiet gut sense before you reach outwards for answers and affirmation.

It may be that you end up somewhere you never expected, somewhere that is more aligned with your values and character than if you'd staunchly followed the step-by-step plan you'd laid out for your life. As you begin to trust that you can only steer your ship, you cannot control the waves, you loosen your grip on control and welcome the opportunity for adventure and possibilities!

Today's energy levels:

Decision I'm Proud Of

The decision I made:

Reflection on my decision:

How to move forward:

Decision I'd Like to Have Made Differently

The decision I made:

Reflection on my decision:

How to move forward:

Did Guilt Feature in My Day?

Address:

Compassion:

Tweak:

Tomorrow's intention:

Day 34

Cast your mind back over your day and, with a gently enquiring mind, think about the moments in which you've held something or someone else responsible for a decision you made. Perhaps you blamed the person who cut you up at the roundabout for your tirade of rage, or your kid for disrupting your sleep, leading you to be short with a colleague.

At the end of the day, there will be many factors at play, both internal and external, that increase your impulsivity or hamper your strength in making good decisions when the opportunities arise. But, in truth, the power to decide how to respond is in your hands only. This personal responsibility can feel like an uncomfortable truth at times, but in taking accountability, you're more likely to search for those supportive habits and conversations.

In the moments you realize you've placed the blame or responsibility elsewhere, pause. Instead of self-blame, which keeps you stuck, opt for self-forgiveness, which frees you up. Instead of allocating the responsibility for your actions to someone else, recognize that you have the option to take responsibility for what you do next.

If you are carrying any residual guilt from the day as you reflect back, work through the ACT three-step technique for guilt. Address the guilt by naming it. Introduce some compassionate words to loosen any shame and let that guilt prompt you to tweak a behaviour or seek support. Then, let that guilt go like a helium balloon on a warm breeze.

Today's energy levels:

Decision I'm Proud Of

The decision I made:

Reflection on my decision:

How to move forward:

Decision I'd Like to Have Made Differently

The decision I made:

Reflection on my decision:

How to move forward:

Did Guilt Feature in My Day?

Address:

Compassion:

Tweak:

Tomorrow's intention:

Day 35

Today is the final day of your guided journalling. Take a moment to reflect on how your feelings towards decision-making and growth have shifted and changed over the course of *The Good Decision Diary*. Do you feel you make decisions – big and small – differently today than you did a few short weeks ago?

In the day to day, it may well seem like little has changed, so it's valuable to look back over the words you've written to notice the small changes, the fruits of your intentions and the power of observing yourself without judgement.

What beneficial decision did you make today that would be so easy to reduce or dismiss? Acknowledge that, from the outside, the decision may have looked small, but for you it required effort and intention, and is therefore something worth celebrating. Notice also any decision that you found really hard, one where everything inside of you resisted. Is this a common theme for you in this sort of decision? If you are often meeting resistance in this area, yet yearn to move forward, question whether your aim is realistic and that support network adequate? If nothing changes, nothing changes.

How have you approached opportunities to slow down and rest as you've moved through each day? Have you overlooked them or welcomed them? How has this helped or hindered your ability to make those nurturing decisions? Rest is the antidote to burnout, and while our culture might applaud you for living frazzled, taking time to slow down and reflect and absorb what you've been through is a way to recoup strength for the decisions that lie ahead.

Today's energy levels:

Decision I'm Proud Of

The decision I made:

Reflection on my decision:

How to move forward:

Decision I'd Like to Have Made Differently

The decision I made:

Reflection on my decision:

How to move forward:

Did Guilt Feature in My Day?

Address:

Compassion:

Tweak:

Tomorrow's intention:

Final Words

It's my hope that the end of *The Good Decision Diary* marks the beginning of so much more for you. Having spent weeks considering the big and small decisions that shape your growth and your path, spend a moment now thinking about how you might continue onwards. Consider how you have reframed your understanding of growth as you've read and reflected. Hopefully you've begun to lean into your gut a little more, and lean on others more too. How might you continue to lean in and on, and what accountability might benefit you to ensure you're having those open, therapeutic conversations?

The intention of making more good decisions more of the time isn't a one-off pledge to yourself, but an ongoing gentle observation of who and how you are, what you need, what goals and hopes might have to be readdressed, where to push forward, when to slow down and pull back, and who you need beside you as you walk through life.

Making good decisions more of the time is about reinserting humanness back into your plans and goals where culture's 'quick-fix schemes' have stripped it away. It's about finding patience for yourself as you grow and meander your way through life, rather than using harsh criticism to direct your steps.

Making good decisions more of the time is an acknowledgement that you'll still inevitably make bad ones. You'll self-sabotage, you'll plough your way knowingly into destructive choices because old narratives can run deep, because tiredness and depletion can pull the strings and the inner critic can be loud. But, at those times, you know you can choose to hit the reset button, cut yourself some slack and perhaps make a different choice next time.

At the end of the day, life is short. It's wonderful and painful; it's a rainbow of greys as you embrace the messy middle between the harsh black and the stark white. Life may flow smoothly for a season and then find you floundering in its choppy waves. Time carries you along, and while it might be easy to proclaim 'You only live once' as a way to justify decisions that hinder your tomorrow, I hope this book acts as an invitation to make better decisions to nurture your tomorrow instead. Decisions that will strengthen your confidence little by little, that will reflect your values and find you living more authentically and fully. Sure, you only live once, so why not make decisions that push into purpose, connection and wholehearted living within the boundaries you place and the spaces in which you choose to invest your precious energy?

My hope is that as you've woven your way through *The Good Decision Diary*, adding more and more of your own words, you have found more acceptance, patience, grace and gentle enquiry towards yourself. My hope is that your goals and plans have become more flexible and open rather than brittle and fixed, and that you keep hopping off the tightrope of right or wrong whenever you realize you've climbed back on to it.

You are the tree, strengthened by the roots beneath the surface. Your branches are a home for wildlife, your leaves healthy and strong. At first glance, the roots are tangled. Some hair-strand thin, some thicker than your thigh. Some are shrivelled, some are wound around rocks. Some reach out further than your eye can see, whereas others stop abruptly, halted by a small pebble nestled in the soil.

When you find yourself questioning whether one unhelpful decision, one seemingly failed attempt to grow in a particular direction, or one slow plod of attempt to change have scuppered you completely, cast your gaze up at the tree again and see the bigger picture of the tree itself.

Take note of how all the trying, the reassessing, the rerouting, has brought you to the here and now. Consider the good and thriving things in your life that are the result of amazing decisions, but also recognize the truth that many of the most precious things in your life happened regardless of the decisions you made, without your effort. It's not all down to you, and neither should it be. You are wired for connection and community, and sometimes you need someone to help you dig down and move the big stones that block your path.

Keep on keeping on. Keep pressing the reset button. Keep listening in to that quiet voice that recognizes the needs over the wants. Keep leaning on others. Keep growing as you go. And, most importantly, keep making those nurturing decisions, more of the time.

Helpful Contacts

CALM – Campaign Against Living Miserably

https://www.thecalmzone.net
A helpline for those in the UK who are feeling down for any reason.

Cruse

https://www.cruse.org.uk
Bereavement support charity, offering free support to those who have lost a loved one.

Depression UK

http://depressionuk.org
A national self-help organization helping people cope with depression.

Help Guide

https://www.helpguide.org
Helping people make changes to improve their mental health.

The Hub of Hope

https://hubofhope.co.uk
Enter your postcode to find local support networks and charities.

Mind

https://www.mind.org.uk
Providing advice and support to empower anyone experiencing a mental health challenge.

The Samaritans

https://www.samaritans.org
Volunteers available to listen every moment of every day.

You can also call 116123 and speak to a trained volunteer day or night.

References

p. 189 Buchan, M. (2012). *Over It: How to Live Above Your Circumstances and Beyond Yourself.* AuthorHouse.

p. 151 Eiseley, L. (1968). 'The Star Thrower'. In *The Unexpected Universe* (pp. 57–70). University of Nebraska Press. (Renewed 1996 by John A. Eichman, III.)

p. 105 Johnson, S. (3 May 1751). *The Rambler,* No. 133.

p. 137 Lounsbrough, C. D. (2014). *An Intimate Collision: Encounters with Life and Jesus.* CreateSpace Independent Publishing Platform.

p. 147 Sandberg, S. (2013). *Lean In: Women, Work, and the Will to Lead.* Alfred A. Knopf.

p. 113 Tolle, E. (2005). *A New Earth: Awakening to Your Life's Purpose.* Plume.

Acknowledgements

How lovely it is to have the opportunity to thank everyone who played a part in getting this book into your hands! Writing a book extends far beyond the solitary hours spent typing at a laptop – it truly takes a community of patient family members and skilled professionals who 'get' my heart and vision.

To my family: thank you for your understanding and encouragement during my creative bursts. When I'm in the writing zone, I work quickly and intensely, with my mind full of words and my attention a bit scattered! Your unwavering support means the world to me. To my husband and children, thank you for always cheering me on from the sidelines with pride.

I still can't believe this is my sixth book and my fourth under the care of the Penguin Life team. To my editor, Pippa, I am so grateful for your grace and trust as we reimagined this book together. What began as a guided journal evolved into something much more expansive

ACKNOWLEDGEMENTS

when I realized I had so many words to share on decision-making. Thank you for letting me run with that inspiration and for skilfully refining my ideas along the way. I'm so proud of what we've created.

To Tom, my literary agent at Bev James: thank you, yet again, for being a confident advocate for my work and for believing in my ability to write from the heart. And to Karen, my copy-editor: your talent for honing my meandering thoughts into something polished and cohesive is unmatched.

Thank you to the journalists, press outlets and media platforms who have championed my work over the years. Your openness to sharing my ideas and words is such a gift. And to the Penguin PR and Marketing team: your dedication to amplifying my voice and helping readers find my words is so appreciated.

And finally, my deepest thanks to you – yes, you! Thank you for taking a chance on my book. I hope it marks the beginning of something wonderful for you. May you discover fresh intention for the decisions you face and embrace a new level of self-compassion and understanding as you choose.